ADVANCE PRAISE FOR

Beyond Labels: Understanding Refugee Students with Disabilities in Educational Contexts

"*Beyond Labels: Understanding Refugee Students with Disabilities in Educational Contexts* is a profoundly important contribution to inclusive education, reflecting both academic rigor and deep humanity. This book challenges us to move beyond simplified notions of inclusion and embrace the complexity and possibility of educational spaces that truly serve all learners. Through compelling case studies and actionable insights, Dr. Warsi offers a vital, enduring resource for teacher educators, school leaders, and policy makers. I especially appreciate how this work illuminates the experiences of refugee children with disabilities, a population too often overlooked, reminding us of their resilience and their right to equitable, responsive, and affirming educational opportunities."

Dr. Carolyn Theard-Griggs,
Dean and Professor, National College of Education,
National Louis University

"In an era of global displacement and political instability, Dr. Warsi's *Beyond Labels: Understanding Refugee Students with Disabilities in Educational Contexts* provides essential guidance for educators. Through detailed case studies of seven students, Dr. Warsi illuminates how young refugees carry the weight of war, displacement, and systemic exclusion, often compounded by educational practices. She demonstrates how students' learning needs are inseparable from the political crises they've fled and the new precarity they face: hostile policies, under-resourced schools, and unprepared systems. This text guides educators to understand how trauma, resilience, cultural knowledge, and disability intersect beyond traditional frameworks, revealing rich pedagogical possibilities through culturally responsive teaching approaches for educational justice."

Blanca Gamez-Djokic, PhD,
Assistant Professor EDD Teaching & Learning,
National College of Education

"Dr. Warsi's groundbreaking text addresses the intersection of disability, cultural diversity, and forced displacement in contemporary education. Through compelling case studies, including Amira, a Bosnian Muslim war refugee and amputee with dyslexia requiring comprehensive support, the author illuminates multilayered challenges facing educators. *Beyond Labels: Understanding Refugee Students with Dis-*

abilities in Educational Contexts provides essential guidance for supporting refugee and migrant children with disabilities from diverse cultural and faith backgrounds. The research-based approach incorporates culturally responsive pedagogical frameworks while offering practical implementation strategies. Dr. Warsi's scholarship bridges critical gaps in educational literature, making this resource invaluable for practitioners serving increasingly diverse student populations with complex needs."

Shabana Mir, PhD
Associate Professor of Anthropology,
American Islamic College, Chicago, IL

"Dr. Warsi addresses a critical resource gap for teachers navigating complex educational terrain with inadequate guidance. This book serves educators who genuinely seek to understand their diverse students. Beginning with her authentic voice, Dr. Warsi then illuminates the lived realities of seven children, offering valuable insights into refugee students' experiences. These real-life narratives demonstrate the profound impact of warm, inclusive environments on displaced children. Dr. Warsi's book, *Beyond Labels: Understanding Refugee Students with Disabilities in Educational Contexts*, is essential reading for public school educators and teacher candidates nationwide. I eagerly anticipate implementing this resource in my own classroom instruction."

Seema A. Imam, EdD, Professor,
National Louis University, National College of Education,
School of Teacher Preparation, Chicago, IL

"If there were a more timely publication on the topic of refugee students and their educational needs, I know of none. The crisis of displaced children spans continents, demanding immediate attention from educators worldwide. *Beyond Labels: Understanding Refugee Students with Disabilities in Educational Contexts* transforms understanding by examining refugee experiences across Asia, Africa, Southeastern Europe and Middle East, with pioneering focus on children with disabilities, a critically underserved population. Teachers, school psychologists, and counselors will discover powerful insights into students' rich cultural backgrounds and evidence-based strategies for providing essential educational and social-emotional support. This vital roadmap creates inclusive environments where refugee students truly thrive."

Robert D. Clark, PhD,
Emeritus Professor, School & International Psychology,
The Chicago School of Professional Psychology, Chicago, IL

Beyond Labels

Beyond Labels

Understanding Refugee Students with Disabilities in Educational Contexts

By Sadia Warsi

Myers Education Press

GORHAM, MAINE

Myers Education Press

Published by Myers Education Press, LLC
P.O. Box 424 Gorham, ME 04038

Myers Education Press is an academic publisher specializing in books, e-books, and digital content in the field of education. All of our books are subjected to a rigorous peer review process and produced in compliance with the standards of the Council on Library and Information Resources.

Library of Congress Cataloging-in-Publication Data available from Library of Congress.

13-digit ISBN 978-1-9755-0923-1 (paperback)
13-digit ISBN 978-1-9755-0924-8 (library networkable e-edition)
13-digit ISBN 978-1-9755-0924-8 (consumer e-edition)

Printed in the United States of America.

All first editions printed on acid-free paper that meets the American National Standards Institute Z39-48 standard.

Books published by Myers Education Press may be purchased at special quantity discount rates for groups, workshops, training organizations, and classroom usage. Please call our customer service department at 1-800-232-0223 for details.

Cover design by Teresa Lagrange.
Cover image by istock/FatCamera.

Visit us on the web at **www.myersedpress.com** to browse our complete list of titles.

DEDICATION

I DEDICATE THIS BOOK to the countless lives touched by displacement and those who stand beside them.

In the quiet hours before dawn, when bombs have momentarily ceased, a family gathers their few possessions and begins a journey into uncertainty. Their story is one of countless others. Refugees whose courage carries them across treacherous borders in search of safety and dignity.

In these same dangerous zones, relief workers move purposefully through rubble, extending hands of compassion where governments have failed. They build shelters from destruction and offer medicine when hospitals have been reduced to dust.

Beside them, journalists crouch with cameras and notepads, documenting atrocities that the world might otherwise forget. Their lenses and pens become weapons against indifference, ensuring that distance cannot excuse our ignorance.

Back in safer lands, writers transform these witnessed truths into narratives that reach into comfortable homes and shake complacent hearts. Their stories bridge impossible distances, making strangers into neighbors we cannot ignore.

And finally, in classrooms both makeshift and permanent, teachers create spaces where interrupted childhoods can resume. They hang colorful drawings on walls still marked by trauma and whisper possibilities into ears that have heard too much violence.

This book exists because of all of you. Those who flee, those who help, those who witness, those who write, and those who teach. May these pages honor your courage, your service, your truth, your words, and your hope.

CONTENTS

ACKNOWLEDGMENTS

WRITING THIS BOOK HAS been a profound personal and professional journey, one that would not have been possible without the support, wisdom, and generosity of so many.

First and foremost, I want to express my deepest gratitude to refugee families everywhere. Your fight for your children's futures and homelands is the most noble feat. Your resilience and commitment to your children's education is an ongoing source of inspiration.

To my daughter, Sophie, a sophomore at Northwestern's Medill School of Journalism, double-majoring in Journalism and Psychology with a minor in Creative Writing, I am in awe of your ability to seamlessly juggle late-night article writing, intense study sessions, and marathon *Words with Friends* games while I worked on this book. Your late nights of studying and writing alongside my own writing journey created a beautiful shared rhythm of academic dedication and playful connection. I look forward to our next book together, whether it's one of yours or one we collaborate on.

To my late Ammi, Azra Warsi, through your strength, I found my own. Through your profound compassion for humanity, I discovered my life's purpose. Your love taught me that true education is about understanding the human spirit, about seeing the dignity in every person's story. Though you are no longer with me, your wisdom continues to guide my path and illuminate the pages of this book.

To my Abbu, Dr. Shaukat Ali Warsi, while I did not follow your path as a mathematics professor, I know you see our shared academic calling as a continuation of the same noble pursuit. Your life taught me that education is not about the discipline we teach, but about the lives we transform.

To my husband, Kamran Memon, your willingness to eat takeout for weeks on end without complaint should earn you some kind of spouse medal. You somehow knew exactly when a bowl of chocolate mocha or a bag of extra-spicy chips would restore my writing mojo better than any pep talk.

I am most grateful for my students in special education who have chosen a profession serving children with disabilities. Your dedication to creating inclusive learning environments, often in the face of resource constraints and systemic barriers, is truly remarkable.

To my colleagues in special education and across the university, your scholarship and tireless advocacy have paved the way for this work. I am particularly indebted to the mentors who have guided my development as a scholar and educator.

To all my besties, thank you for the support, laughter, and perspective throughout this journey. Your friendship has been a source of strength and joy.

It is my hope that the insights and strategies shared in these pages will contribute to creating more inclusive, equitable, and affirming educational environments for all students, especially those at the intersections of displacement and disability.

"Say, 'My Lord, increase me in knowledge.'" (Quran 20:114)

PREFACE

THE INTERSECTION OF DISABILITY, education, cultural diversity, and forced displacement represents one of the most complex yet underexplored areas in educational research and practice. When a refugee student with a disability enters a classroom, they bring with them a unique constellation of experiences, challenges, and strengths that many educators feel underprepared to support. The intersection of these identities creates educational needs that extend far beyond what current literature or teacher preparation programs typically address. This gap in understanding and resources leaves both teachers and students struggling to navigate complex terrain with inadequate maps.

According to recent global estimates, more than 82 million people worldwide have been forcibly displaced from their homes due to conflict, persecution, and human rights violations. Among these, approximately 26 million are refugees who have crossed international borders seeking safety. Within this already vulnerable population, disabled refugees face compounded challenges that often remain invisible within both refugee services and disability support systems. The World Health Organization suggests that the prevalence of disability among refugee populations often exceeds that of general populations, with rates estimated between 15% and 20% compared to the global average of 15%. Despite these significant numbers, research and practical guidance addressing the educational needs of refugee students with disabilities remain notably sparse.

Numbers alone cannot capture the lived experiences of these students or guide educators in meeting their needs. Behind each statistic is a young person trying to learn while managing the compound challenges of disability, cultural adjustment, language acquisition, and often trauma. Their stories demand not only our attention but our commitment to creating educational environments that recognize and nurture their full humanity.

The educational barriers facing refugee students with disabilities are multilayered and complex. Language acquisition, often positioned as the primary challenge for refugee students, becomes further complicated when intertwined with learning disabilities, sensory disabilities, or mental health conditions resulting from traumatic experiences. Cultural understandings of disability that differ from dominant Western medical models can create misunderstandings between families and educational systems. Access to appropriate assistive technologies, specialized interventions, and inclusive educational environments may be limited by resource constraints, communication barriers, and systemic gaps in service provision. These challenges exist within broader societal contexts often marked by xenophobia, ableism, and other forms of discrimination that further marginalize students at these intersections.

As a professor of special education for over two decades, I bring a unique perspective to these intersections. My journey as a visibly Muslim woman in Western academia has been marked by challenges, revelations, and a deepening commitment to social justice and inclusive education. Throughout my 20-plus years in higher education, I have witnessed firsthand how teacher preparation programs have evolved and where they continue to fall short in addressing the complex needs of diverse learners. My academic work explores the intersections between literacy development, diversity, and inclusive teaching practices, informed by my experiences navigating multiple cultural, religious, and professional identities.

My path as an educator and researcher has been profoundly influenced by my family background in academia, my educational experiences across multiple countries, and my interest in supporting underrepresented students. Growing up across India, Iraq, Canada, and Saudi Arabia gave me firsthand experience understanding diverse cultures, religions, and international education systems. This global upbringing provided a foundation for appreciating different perspectives and recognizing how educational approaches vary across contexts.

As an elementary school student, I lived through the devastating war between Iraq and Iran. During this difficult time, my father, a professor at Mosul University, had to leave his job due to the escalating conflict. Our family was forced to leave our home for our safety, which meant abandoning everything familiar. This abrupt displacement led us to Canada, where both my parents worked tirelessly to reestablish our family's life. My father, once a respected university professor, navigated the challenges of rebuilding his academic career, while my mother, who held a master's degree in Urdu literature, channeled her intellectual passion and academic dreams into a profound commitment to her children's education.

This personal experience with displacement provided me with insights into educational disruption that academic study alone could never offer. I understand viscerally what it means to leave behind not just a home, but an educational identity and to enter new learning environments where previous knowledge may be discounted or invisible, where linguistic barriers create false perceptions of academic abilities, and where the emotional impact of displacement affects every aspect of learning and development.

Two years before the COVID-19 pandemic started, I volunteered to tutor young Syrian refugee children after school in my neighborhood school and befriend their families. These relationships added immeasurably to my understanding and respect for the families and their sacrifices. Through these connections, I witnessed firsthand the extraordinary resilience, determination, and hope that refugee families maintain despite unimaginable challenges. Their willingness to share their stories and experiences profoundly shaped my perspective on what meaningful educational support truly entails, showing me how cultural knowledge, family wisdom, and community strength serve as essential foundations for educational success.

These personal and professional experiences have shaped my approach to educational research and practice, fueling my commitment to creating more inclusive and responsive educational spaces for students navigating similar transitions.

Throughout my academic career, I have been drawn to work that addresses gaps in educational research and practice, particularly at the intersections of disability, cultural diversity, and marginalization. My research has explored how literacy development is shaped by cultural and linguistic factors, how inclusive teaching practices can be adapted to diverse learning contexts, and how educator preparation programs can better equip teachers to serve students with complex, intersectional identities. This work has consistently revealed the need for more nuanced, culturally responsive approaches to disability in educational settings, particularly for students from refugee backgrounds.

This book developed from my work teaching graduate classes to special education teacher candidates who consistently asked for more opportunities to learn about diverse children, especially children who are refugees with disabilities who will be arriving in their classrooms. Year after year, I witnessed passionate, committed educators in training express both eagerness to serve these students effectively and anxiety about their limited preparation for this complex work. They sought concrete examples, practical strategies, and deeper understanding of the lived experiences of refugee students with disabilities.

While many excellent texts address either refugee education or disability in education separately, few examine their intersection. Research on refugee education often treats disability as a peripheral consideration, while disability studies typically does not deeply engage with the specific contexts of forced migration and cultural displacement. Even fewer resources provide practical guidance for educators working at this crossroads, leaving teachers to improvise approaches that may inadvertently reinforce rather than address barriers to educational equity.

The case studies presented in this book aim to address this gap by providing detailed explorations of the educational experiences of refugee students with various disabilities. Each narrative examines the complex interplay between cultural background, displacement experiences, and specific disability-related needs, offering educators windows into the multifaceted realities their students may be navigating. Importantly, these case studies move beyond deficit-focused approaches to highlight the strengths, resources, and resilience these students bring to educational settings.

The case studies presented in this book intentionally span a diverse range of disabilities, representing the complex landscape that educators may encounter in their classrooms. Through Amira, we explore the intersection of physical disabilities (amputation) and learning disabilities (dyslexia), highlighting how multiple disability categories can create unique educational considerations. Amir's story examines autism spectrum disorder in the context of detention, illustrating how sensory processing differences and communication challenges are exacerbated by institutional environments. Zahra's experience with traumatic brain injury allows us to consider how acquired cognitive disabilities affect memory, attention, processing speed, and executive functioning during educational transitions. Noor's selective mutism presents a window into communication disorders that intertwine with trauma responses and cultural displacement. The siblings Adam and Aya demonstrate how different disability types (Adam's cerebral palsy and Aya's epilepsy) manifest within the same family system and cultural context. Finally, Maha's visual impairment highlights the challenges of sensory disabilities when educational materials and environments remain inaccessible.

By examining this breadth of disability categories (physical, cognitive, developmental, neurological, sensory, and communication), the book provides a comprehensive framework for understanding how different types of disabilities interact with the refugee experience. This diversity is intentional, reflecting the reality that educators need flexible, multifaceted approaches rather than simplified solutions. Each disability creates distinct educational barriers but also cultivates unique strengths and adaptive strategies that can inform more responsive educational practices.

It is important to note that while the case studies presented in this book are not based on these Syrian families I worked with, nor taken directly from specific novels on refugees or disability memoirs, they are deeply inspired by my continuous engagement with literature in both areas, the never-ending news about conflicts that create refugees, reports from refugee relief organizations who are on the ground sharing their experiences, and refugees themselves sharing their loss and grief on social media when mainstream media would not cover their stories. As an educator and scholar, I am constantly immersed in novels, memoirs, and academic works by authors who write about refugee experiences, disability narratives, and the intersection of these identities. The extensive list of references at the end of this book reflects the breadth of literary and scholarly works that have informed my understanding and shaped the development of these composite narratives.

The approach taken in this book draws intentionally from both academic research and literary representations of refugee and disability experiences. By weaving together insights from empirical studies, theoretical frameworks, and the rich tapestry of lived experiences depicted in literature, I aim to create case studies that are simultaneously grounded in reality and evocative of the human dimensions of these intersectional experiences. This integration of academic and literary approaches reflects my belief that effective educational practice must be informed by both rigorous research and deep empathetic engagement with diverse human stories.

This book serves as both a practical resource and a call to action for educators, researchers, and policymakers. It aims to transform educational spaces by providing tools for understanding and supporting refugee students with disabilities, while advocating for systemic changes that better serve these interconnected communities. Through deep engagement with these intersecting experiences, the book invites educators to reimagine inclusive education and work toward learning environments that honor the full humanity of every student.

My hope is that these case studies will spark meaningful conversations, inform thoughtful practice, and inspire creative approaches to supporting refugee students with disabilities. Beyond providing practical strategies, I aim to nurture a vision of educational spaces where differences are not merely accommodated but valued, where multiple forms of knowledge and communication are recognized, and where all students can develop their unique capabilities in communities of belonging. This vision requires more than technical adjustments to existing educational systems; it demands a fundamental rethinking of how we understand disability, cultural diversity, and educational purpose in an increasingly interconnected yet unequal world.

INTRODUCTION

The Intersection of Displacement and Disability:

A Critical Educational Imperative

In classrooms across the globe, a growing number of students navigate the profound challenge of rebuilding their educational futures after forced displacement. Among these young people are those who also experience disability, creating an intersection of vulnerability and strength that demands our urgent attention as educators. This convergence of refugee experience and disability represents one of education's most pressing yet under-addressed challenges.

The Scale and Significance of the Challenge

According to the United Nations High Commissioner for Refugees (UNHCR, 2023), there are approximately 103 million forcibly displaced people worldwide, including over 32.5 million refugees who have fled across international borders seeking safety from persecution, conflict, or violence. Within this population, global estimates suggest that at least 15% have disabilities, a percentage likely higher in forced displacement contexts due to conflict-related injuries, limited healthcare access, and environmental barriers. This translates to over 4.8 million refugees with disabilities, including hundreds of thousands of school-age children.

The urgency of addressing their needs cannot be overstated. Without appropriate educational supports, these students risk becoming part of what humanitarian researchers have termed a "lost generation," children whose potential remains unrealized due to disrupted education and compounding barriers. As one mother explained in research by Humanity & Inclusion (2017):

> My children have grown up amid war. The sort of travels they have been through, full of misery and death, have nothing to do with what I experienced as a child. They have seen people die. They have not been able to go to school. They do not know peace and safety. Their fear makes your heart ache.

A Framework for Understanding Disability in Displacement Contexts

The intersection of displacement and disability manifests in distinct ways depending on the nature of the disability, creating unique challenges for educational systems. This book examines a spectrum of disability types to provide a comprehensive understanding of how different disabilities interact with forced migration experiences.

Physical disabilities in displacement contexts often face escalating barriers as familiar accommodations, assistive devices, and accessible environments are lost during flight. Imagine a child who uses mobility aids navigating the uneven terrain of a refugee camp, or a student with fine motor challenges attempting to complete written work without adapted materials. The physical environments of temporary housing, camps, or under-resourced schools present daily navigational challenges that compound educational barriers.

Developmental disabilities create distinct social, communication, and sensory processing challenges that are frequently misinterpreted in displacement contexts. The need for predictability and routine, essential for many children with developmental disabilities, directly conflicts with the unpredictable nature of forced migration. Language acquisition difficulties may mask underlying neurodevelopmental differences, leading to missed opportunities for appropriate intervention.

Acquired cognitive disabilities, such as those resulting from traumatic brain injury, affect memory, attention, processing speed, and executive functioning in ways that complicate educational transitions. A student struggling with cognitive processing challenges may be misunderstood as simply having difficulty with a new language, when in fact their needs extend beyond language acquisition support.

Communication disorders become especially complex when overlaid with trauma responses and cross-cultural transitions. When silence or communication differences are interpreted through cultural lenses or attributed solely to language barriers, the underlying communication needs may go unrecognized and unaddressed.

Sensory impairments create particular vulnerabilities during displacement, as environmental cues change abruptly and navigational strategies developed in familiar settings no longer apply. Educational materials in accessible formats may be unavailable, and specialized technologies often remain inaccessible in temporary or under-resourced educational settings.

Medical conditions requiring consistent management present life-threatening risks during displacement as medication regimens are disrupted and healthcare access becomes sporadic. The educational implications extend beyond immediate health concerns to include cognitive impacts and safety considerations that must be addressed in learning environments.

These various disability categories require differentiated approaches to educational support, yet all share common themes of accessibility, cultural context, trauma-informed practice, and the critical importance of family partnerships. By examining this range of disabilities through detailed case studies, educators can develop more nuanced, responsive approaches that recognize both the unique challenges and the remarkable adaptations that emerge at this intersection.

Throughout the book, this framework helps illuminate how disability-specific barriers interact with the broader challenges of displacement, cultural transition, and educational disruption. It allows us to move beyond generalized approaches to develop more targeted, effective strategies for supporting refugee students with disabilities in achieving their full educational potential.

The Psychological Impact of Displacement

The challenges faced by refugee students with disabilities extend far beyond physical access. Research consistently documents the profound psychological impacts of forced displacement, including loss of dignity, identity disruption, and social isolation. For individuals with disabilities, these psychological dimensions can be particularly acute.

The Humanity & Inclusion study on Syrian refugees found that the combination of fear, stress, and distress was identified as the third most important collective effect of explosive weapons use in Syria. For women, it was the second most significant effect, with 61% of female respondents citing fear as the primary effect, compared to 37% of men. Female interviewees also consistently mentioned the long-term impact of fear on themselves and their children (Humanity & Inclusion, 2017, p. 36).

The loss of dignity was reported by almost half (45%) of respondents with bombing-related disabilities. As one participant stated, "Forced migration is humiliating. Need is humiliating; living in a community that is not your own is also humiliating. We have a popular saying: those who leave their homes lose their worth. It is a suffering that cannot be described in words; words cannot describe the horror we have been through" (Humanity & Inclusion, 2017, p. 5).

For those who acquire disabilities during conflict or displacement, the psychological impact of new dependency can be overwhelming. One woman who became paralyzed after being shot explained, "My sons had to carry me; my children had to move me. I feel humiliated. I cannot go to the bathroom by myself" (Humanity & Inclusion, 2017, p. 33). For 30% of respondents with conflict-related disabilities, loss of independence was cited as the primary effect of displacement, caused by dependence on aid, disruptions in access to services, and restrictions in unfamiliar environments.

The disorientation and loss of identity that accompanies forced displacement was captured poignantly by another refugee:

> For a full eight months, we lived a life of running and constant escape. We no longer had a home. We no longer had our family around us. We had no place to go. We were two women alone . . . Not having a home was a very scary feeling for me, I felt lost. Your home is your dignity. Home is where your family is . . . There was no destination. Damascus, where we went first, was not the destination. Lebanon, where we ended up, was not the destination. The destination was safety and security. This is the only thing we were looking for but we did not know where it was. I did not find it. (Humanity & Inclusion, 2017, p. 38)

The psychological impact on children is particularly pronounced. One mother described: "My daughter was always afraid. She wet the bed out of fear and she also often peed her pants" (Humanity & Inclusion, 2017, p. 37). Another recounted:

> My children have grown up amid war. The sort of travels they have been through, full of misery and death, have nothing to do with what I experienced

> as a child. They have seen people die. They have not been able to go to school. They do not know peace and safety. Their fear makes your heart ache. (Humanity & Inclusion, 2017, p. 32)

The constant exposure to violence and death creates profound trauma. As one teacher explained:

> I clung to life because I loved myself; I loved my children; I loved my friends; I loved my students; I loved my house, the walls, and the olive trees. I lost my son—he died; my brother died; my student died; my neighbor died; my friend died; my cousin died. Death surrounds you. I am afraid of death and of the thought that at any moment I might lose my other son, my mother, or my loved ones. (Humanity & Inclusion, 2017, p. 21)

Heightened Vulnerability and Risk

The intersection of refugee status and disability creates specific vulnerabilities that demand urgent attention from educational systems. Research by UNHCR emphasizes that "persons with disabilities experience violence at much higher rates than persons without disabilities and may experience targeted violence and abuse on the basis of disability" (UNHCR, 2019, p. 19). This targeted violence can include physical abuse, denial of food and medicine, harassment, emotional abuse, and profound neglect, often perpetrated by persons known to them.

According to UNHCR guidance, this violence may specifically target individuals based on their disability status. This includes both generalized violence in conflict settings that disproportionately affects persons with disabilities, as well as targeted attacks and abuses directed at them because of their disability (UNHCR, 2019).

Children with disabilities are particularly vulnerable in displacement contexts. According to UNHCR,

> children with disabilities are almost four times more likely to become victims of violence than are children without disabilities. More than one in four have been subjected to some form of violence, and one in five is a victim of physical violence. (UNHCR, 2019, p. 19)

In conflict and displacement contexts, these risks are further magnified by the breakdown of protective systems and community networks.

Sexual and gender-based violence (SGBV) also disproportionately affects persons with disabilities. Men, women, boys, and girls with disabilities face heightened risk of SGBV due to misconceptions about disability, social isolation, and loss of protective community networks (Women's Refugee Commission, 2013). Girls and young women with disabilities are more likely to experience violence than either their male peers with disabilities or girls and young women without disabilities (UNHCR, 2019). Despite being at heightened risk, persons with disabilities are often overlooked in SGBV prevention and response programs due to inaccessible information, reporting and communication barriers, and lack of awareness among service providers (Women's Refugee Commission, 2015).

UNHCR notes that certain populations face compounded vulnerabilities. Persons with intellectual and psychosocial disabilities often face particularly high levels of stigma, resulting in heightened risk of exploitation and abuse due to isolation, lack of access to services, and negative community perceptions (UNHCR, 2019). In many contexts, children with intellectual and psychosocial disabilities are excluded from education and may be hidden from view, restrained inside their homes, or institutionalized.

Multiple Displacements and Disrupted Development

The journey of displacement for many refugee families is rarely a direct path from danger to safety. Research documents that families often experience multiple displacements before reaching relative security. Among Syrian refugees surveyed in one major study by Humanity & Inclusion (formerly Handicap International), almost half had been internally displaced prior to seeking external refuge, with an average of three internal displacements within their own city. In addition to displacement within their own city, the majority had been displaced between one to three different Syrian cities before crossing borders (Humanity & Inclusion, 2017).

When asked about what drove their forced displacements, the most common reply by men and women alike was bombing and shelling (36% of all respondents). Among respondents with bombing-related disabilities, an even higher percentage (45%) identified bombing and shelling as the primary driver for their forced displacement (Humanity & Inclusion, 2017, p. 8).

As one Syrian woman reflected:

> When the bombing followed us everywhere . . . We went to KA, a small town a one-hour drive to the west. Five days later, we went back to our home in D. It was horrible. Everything had been destroyed . . . We returned to KA and stayed there a few months (five or six), but soon fighting started there as well. There were explosions on all sides, it was coming from everywhere: rockets, bombing, shooting, airplanes, and fighting between groups all around us. We were caught in the middle of it all with no place to hide. (Humanity & Inclusion, 2017, p. 14)

For children with physical disabilities, interrupted physical therapy and lack of appropriate mobility devices can lead to contractures, muscle weakness, and secondary complications that create permanent limitations. As one Syrian refugee mother described her experience:

> I was injured when our house was bombed. My foot was swollen and I had open wounds on my leg. But I did not even have time to get shoes. I walked barefoot for eight hours straight on the first day . . . The infection grew worse during our travels, and now I can barely walk. (Humanity & Inclusion, 2017, p. 28)

For children with sensory impairments, critical periods for intervention may be missed, transforming potentially temporary or manageable conditions into permanent disabilities with lifelong implications. One Syrian woman noted of her son:

> He was taken to a local dispensary . . . they did not have the necessary equipment. They just stitched his wounds without removing the shrapnel inside. It is not their fault; they had no equipment and there were a lot of injured persons. (Humanity & Inclusion, 2017, p. 38)

For children with intellectual or developmental disabilities, the loss of consistent educational and therapeutic interventions during critical developmental windows can have irreversible impacts on cognitive and social functioning.

For children with mental health conditions, appropriate psychiatric care becomes almost impossible to access during repeated displacements, leading to worsening symptoms and missed opportunities for effective treatment. As one Syrian refugee observed: "My daughter was treated for psychiatric disorders caused by the war. The fear is a burden we all carry" (Humanity & Inclusion, 2017, p. 34).

Healthcare Disruption and Educational Implications

The disruption of healthcare services during conflict and displacement has profound implications for educational access and success. Research consistently documents how conflict destroys healthcare infrastructure, disrupts medication supply chains, and forces medical professionals to flee, creating near-impossible conditions for managing health and disability-related needs.

As one young woman described her experience following injury in a bombing:

> My arm got infected and was swollen from inflammation. There was no medicine, nothing . . . The hospital where I was treated was far from a fully-equipped hospital; it was more like a dispensary. They could manage to do some emergency procedures, but they were not equipped with what I needed. Also, it was a scary place. It had been shelled many times. We were all in the basement so that the bombs would not reach us. It still did not feel safe. We knew that it was a target. All hospitals were. (Humanity & Inclusion, 2017, p. 22)

For refugee students with disabilities, these healthcare disruptions directly impact educational participation in multiple ways: Medication for conditions like epilepsy, attention disorders, or psychiatric conditions becomes unavailable or inconsistent, leading to breakthrough symptoms that interfere with learning and school attendance. As one Syrian woman explained: "Once we were under siege, it became impossible to get my medicines. Even antiseptics and painkillers were hard to find" (Humanity & Inclusion, 2017, p. 23).

Assistive devices like hearing aids, glasses, prosthetics, or mobility aids are damaged, lost, or outgrown during displacement with limited options for repair or replacement, creating new barriers to educational access. In some cases, displaced persons create makeshift solutions: "We made a cane out of a piece of wood that we found along the way. When it was too difficult, my husband carried me" (Humanity & Inclusion, 2017, p. 29).

For women, the lack of access to health services is a particularly grave concern, as reproductive health services, including emergency obstetric care, become scarce or nonexistent. As one teacher recounted: "Several women died in childbirth, and several infants died because there were no hospitals nearby to take them to" (Humanity & Inclusion, 2017, p. 5).

These healthcare disruptions transform manageable conditions into significant educational barriers. A student whose seizures were well-controlled in their home country may experience breakthrough seizures due to medication interruptions, creating both medical emergencies and educational disruptions.

Cultural Frameworks of Disability and Education

Understanding the cultural dimensions of disability is essential for supporting refugee students effectively. Different cultural contexts provide varying frameworks for making meaning of disability, shaping how families understand their children's needs and how they approach educational support. These cultural understandings are neither more nor less valid than Western medical or educational models, they represent different ways of making meaning that must be engaged respectfully.

UNHCR's guidance on working with persons with disabilities in forced displacement emphasizes the importance of adopting a rights-based approach rather than a medical or charity model. This rights-based approach recognizes persons with disabilities as active rights holders rather than passive recipients of care, and aligns with the principles of the Convention on the Rights of Persons with Disabilities (CRPD) (UNHCR, 2023).

The UNHCR guidance particularly highlights certain population groups who face specific cultural challenges. For instance, persons with albinism may face severe stigma in some cultural contexts due to misbeliefs and myths that can lead to isolation, discrimination, and even violence. Similarly, persons with intellectual and psychosocial disabilities often face particularly high levels of stigma that can result in exclusion from education, livelihood opportunities, and community leadership roles (UNHCR, 2023).

Palik et al. (2023) have recently highlighted how these cultural frameworks significantly impact educational interventions for refugee children with disabilities. Their scoping review of existing impact evaluations emphasizes that educational approaches must consider not only physical accessibility but also cultural understandings of disability that shape family engagement with educational systems.

Navigating these cultural frameworks requires profound humility from educators. Rather than positioning Western educational approaches as inherently superior, effective practice requires recognizing the wisdom embedded in diverse cultural understandings and building bridges between different knowledge systems. The UNHCR guidance emphasizes the importance of consulting with persons with disabilities on their needs and preferences and involving both persons with disabilities and community leaders in awareness-raising activities to promote positive messages about disability (UNHCR, 2019, p. 13).

This cultural translation process must go beyond simplified cultural competence checklists to engage deeply with the lived experiences and expertise of refugee families.

Resilience and Strength Amid Adversity

While understanding the challenges faced by refugee students with disabilities is crucial, equally important is recognizing their remarkable resilience and strengths. Research consistently documents how refugees with disabilities develop extraordinary adaptive strategies, creative problem-solving approaches, and determination amid seemingly impossible circumstances.

Families and communities demonstrate remarkable resourcefulness in supporting members with disabilities during displacement. They create improvised assistive devices from available materials, develop alternative communication systems when languages change, adapt cultural practices to accommodate disabilities in new contexts, and establish knowledge-sharing networks to navigate complex service systems.

Testimonies from Syrian refugees documented by Humanity & Inclusion illustrate this resilience. One woman explained:

> After [he was injured in the bombing of our house], it took two months before my husband was able to start walking again slowly. People knew my husband could not work, so they would help us; they were wonderful. The war has brought us closer together. But in some other places we went

> to, there was a lot of fear; people did not trust each other. That made everything more difficult; even the bombing felt scarier. (Humanity & Inclusion, 2017, p. 27)

Even in the most challenging circumstances, displaced persons found ways to rebuild livelihoods:

> A neighbour had an olive orchard and he paid us to take care of it. We all worked in it: my husband would help with the watering and the children and I would do other things, like taking care of the trees. (Humanity & Inclusion, 2017, p. 27)

Perhaps most remarkable is the determination to seek treatment and recovery despite seemingly insurmountable obstacles. One young woman injured in a bombing described her journey:

> I felt my face was mutilated because the wound over my eye would not heal. I did not want people to see me. I was ashamed. But I did not want to inspire pity. I wanted to recover my pride and my face. I knew a good surgeon could do that, which is why I left home again for Damascus. By then, the enclave had a network of tunnels. In May 2015, I went through one of them, back to Damascus. (Humanity & Inclusion, 2017, p. 23)

These examples of human ingenuity and collective care challenge deficit-focused narratives that position refugees with disabilities solely as victims rather than as active agents navigating complex circumstances. They remind us that effective educational approaches must build upon these existing strengths and adaptive strategies rather than focusing exclusively on perceived limitations.

The Educational Imperative: Beyond Access to Belonging

The educational needs of refugee students with disabilities extend far beyond basic access. While physical accessibility, language support, and appropriate accommodations form the foundation of educational inclusion, deeper needs for belonging, identity development, and genuine participation must also be addressed.

Recent longitudinal research in Kakuma Refugee Camp challenges simplistic approaches to inclusion, finding that refugee students with disabilities showed different developmental trajectories depending on educational environments. According to Crea et al. (2022), a longitudinal study of 129 students (78 in specialized schools and 51 in mainstream settings) revealed important distinctions between specialized and mainstream educational environments. The study found that specialized settings sometimes provided protective factors for social and behavioral development that were absent in mainstream settings lacking adequate resources (Crea et al., 2022).

Specifically, while children in special needs classrooms initially showed greater difficulties and lower prosocial scores than children in mainstream classrooms, the difference in prosocial behaviors decreased over time. By the follow-up assessment 2.5 years later, children in special needs classrooms had nearly equivalent scores to those in mainstream settings. Similarly, children's behavioral difficulties decreased more rapidly in special needs settings than in mainstream classrooms over the study period (Crea et al., 2022, p. 5).

These protective factors may be attributable to several aspects of specialized educational environments: significantly smaller class sizes with lower teacher-student ratios; classroom environments where all students experience some form of disability, potentially reducing marginalization; and a gradual transition approach that eases children into educational environments.

These findings suggest that what constitutes an "inclusive" environment may look different in displacement contexts than in stable, resource-rich educational systems. In highly resource-constrained contexts like refugee camps, special needs schools may be better equipped to serve children with higher levels of need since teachers can focus specifically on disability-related requirements in smaller, more tailored classroom environments. This perspective has been further developed in Crea et al.'s follow-up research (2023), which emphasizes the importance of contextually appropriate inclusion strategies.

A Call to Educational Action

The intersection of refugee experience and disability creates both an urgent challenge and a profound opportunity for educational systems. By developing approaches that effectively support these students, we not only address the needs of a particularly vulnerable population but strengthen our capacity to create truly inclusive education for all learners.

The challenges are significant: in refugee camps, education access remains limited for all children, with only 68% attending primary school (compared to 91% worldwide) and just 34% attending secondary school (compared to 84% worldwide) (UNHCR, 2021). For children with disabilities, these disparities are even more pronounced due to infrastructure limitations, stigmatization, and inadequate specialized support.

Recent research by Dupuy, Palik, and Østby (2022) has documented how national regulatory frameworks in host countries can create additional barriers to educational access for refugee children. Their study of low- and middle-income host countries identified specific policy constraints that disproportionately affect refugees with disabilities, highlighting the need for targeted advocacy efforts to address these systemic barriers.

Effective educational responses must operate at multiple levels simultaneously and adopt what UNHCR calls a "twin-track approach" that:

1. Designs all responses to be inclusive of and accessible to persons with disabilities, and

2. Includes targeted actions (such as strengthening the capacities of persons with disabilities and providing reasonable accommodation) to enable persons with disabilities to participate on an equal basis (UNHCR, 2023).

This approach should include:

Classroom practices that integrate trauma-informed approaches, culturally responsive teaching, and universal design for learning to create accessible, healing-centered learning environments. This may include developing a graduated system where children with disabilities initially receive education in more supportive specialized settings before transitioning to mainstream classrooms when appropriate. UNHCR guidance emphasizes that "universal design means the design of products, environments, programs and services to be usable by all people, to the greatest extent possible, without the need for adaptation or specialized design" (UNHCR, 2023).

School-wide systems that facilitate coordination between language specialists, special educators, cultural liaisons, and mental health professionals to provide integrated rather than fragmented support. Schools must also address the specific disability types most prevalent among refugee children, which research in Kakuma has identified as primarily cognitive disabilities (45%), followed by self-care disabilities (approximately 25%) and communication disabilities (Crea et al., 2022, p. 5).

Community partnerships that engage refugee families and communities as essential collaborators in educational planning and implementation. This includes addressing stigmatization that occurs not only in schools but also within homes and communities, where families may face blame or isolation due to their child's disability. UNHCR emphasizes building links with organizations of persons with disabilities (DPOs) who can advocate for rights, provide peer support, and help build capacity to improve program accessibility (UNHCR, 2023).

Policy advocacy that addresses systemic barriers in education, healthcare, immigration, and social service systems that create unnecessary hurdles for refugee students with disabilities. This includes providing specialized teacher training, ensuring physical accessibility of learning environments, and creating comprehensive support networks that recognize the unique intersection of refugee status and disability.

Recent joint guidance from UNICEF, UNESCO, and UNHCR (2023) has further developed this framework, providing specific recommendations for building inclusive education systems for refugees with disabilities. Their collaborative brief emphasizes the importance of data collection, teacher training, and systematic accommodation planning to ensure genuine inclusion.

As we engage with these research findings, we are called to recognize both the extraordinary challenges faced by refugee students with disabilities and their remarkable capacity for resilience, growth, and contribution when provided with appropriate support. Their educational success depends not only on specialized techniques or accommodations but on our willingness to create learning environments that honor their full humanity, complex identities, and inherent dignity.

The educational imperative is clear: we must move beyond labels, beyond simplified approaches, to develop responsive, integrated educational practices that support refugee students with disabilities in achieving their full potential. A graduated approach to inclusion may ensure that children's gains are preserved if and when they transition between educational settings.

UNHCR recommends several cross-cutting actions to support this work:

1. Change attitudes about disability and promote respect for diversity. Address negative attitudes and beliefs that are often the most significant barriers to achieving rights and accessing services (UNHCR, 2019).

2. Improve identification and data collection. Use appropriate tools like the Washington Group Short Set of Questions on Disability to identify persons with disabilities, as many are overlooked in registration and assessment processes (UNHCR, 2019).

3. Make all facilities physically accessible. Apply universal design principles so that all spaces and facilities meet the needs of all people, including those with disabilities (UNHCR, 2019).

4. Ensure accountability mechanisms are inclusive. Make information and feedback mechanisms available in multiple and accessible formats so persons with disabilities can access and meaningfully participate (UNHCR, 2019).

5. Prevent and respond to violence and abuse. Establish mechanisms to identify and monitor disability-related violence and provide practical resources to improve physical security (UNHCR, 2019).

6. Build links with organizations of persons with disabilities. Partner with Disabled Persons Organizations (DPOs) who can advocate for rights and provide peer support (UNHCR, 2019).

By implementing twin-tracking strategies that address both individual needs and systemic barriers simultaneously, we can create genuinely inclusive environments that serve the complex needs at the intersection of displacement and disability. UNHCR's 2023 guidance on building inclusive education systems for refugees provides an updated framework for this work, emphasizing the importance of collaboration between education and protection sectors.

The futures of these students, and the future of our increasingly diverse educational communities, depend on our commitment to this essential work.

References

Crea, T. M., Klein, E. K., Okunoren, O., Jimenez, M. P., St. Arnold, G., Kirior, T., Velandria, E., & Bruni, D. (2022). Inclusive education in a refugee camp for children with disabilities: How are school setting and children's behavioral functioning related? *Conflict and Health, 16*(1), Article 53. https://doi.org/10.1186/s13031-022-00486-6

Crea, T. M., Diaz-Valdes, A., Evans, K., Hasson, R. H., Kistner, J., LaMaster, K., Moritz, A. G., Mubarak, R., Nader, L. A., & Rudahindwa, N. (2023). Contextually appropriate inclusion strategies for refugee education. *Journal of Refugee Studies.*

Dupuy, K., Palik, J., & Østby, G. (2022). No right to read: National regulatory restrictions on refugee rights to formal education in low- and middle-income host countries. *International Journal of Educational Development, 88*, Article 102537. https://doi.org/10.1016/j.ijedudev.2021.102537

Humanity & Inclusion. (2017). *Everywhere the bombing followed us: Forced displacement and the use of explosive weapons in populated areas. Perspectives of Syrian women refugees in Lebanon.* Retrieved from https://www.hi-us.org/sn_uploads/document/Everywhere_the_bombing_followed_us_2017_Report.pdf

Palik, J., Dupuy, K., & Østby, G. (2023). Interventions to improve refugee children's access to education and quality learning: A scoping review of existing impact evaluations. *International Review of Education, 69*(1–2), 227–247. https://doi.org/10.1007/s11159-023-10004-2

UNHCR. (2019). *Need to know guidance: Working with persons with disabilities in forced displacement.*

UNHCR. (2021). *Staying the course: The challenges facing refugee education* (UNHCR Education Report 2021).

UNHCR. (2023). Building inclusive education systems for refugees with disabilities.

UNICEF, UNESCO, & UNHCR. (2023). Inclusive education for refugees with disabilities: Joint guidance brief.

Women's Refugee Commission. (2013). Disability inclusion in gender-based violence programming.

Women's Refugee Commission. (2015). *"I see that it is possible": Building capacity for disability inclusion in gender-based violence programming in humanitarian settings.*

Comprehensive Case Studies:

The Intersection of Refugee Experiences and Disability

CHAPTER ONE

Amira:

Navigating Physical Disabilities, Dyslexia, and Displacement in Inclusive Classrooms and Providing Strategies for Accommodation and Empowerment

Background

AMIRA, A 16-YEAR-OLD MUSLIM Bosnian refugee living in Rochester, New York, represents the complex intersection of physical disability, learning disability, forced displacement, and educational adaptation. Her journey from war-torn Sarajevo to an American high school illuminates both the significant challenges faced by students with multiple disabilities in new cultural contexts and the remarkable resilience they can develop. Through Amira's story, we explore how educators can implement strategies that address her physical and learning needs while supporting her cultural transition and language development.

Early Life and Education in Bosnia

Born in Sarajevo to a Muslim family of educators, Amira's early childhood was embedded in a rich cultural context characterized by the city's multicultural heritage and intellectual traditions. Her mother worked as a literature teacher and her father as a history teacher at secondary schools in Sarajevo. Their middle-class urban household valued education deeply, with regular family discussions about literature, history, and current events creating an intellectually stimulating environment despite growing political tensions in the region.

The family lived in an apartment in central Sarajevo, where they were part of a diverse neighborhood community of residents. Before the war, this multicultural coexistence was a source of pride and cultural richness. Amira attended a local elementary school where she was an active, engaged child who participated fully in both formal education and cultural activities in her community. She demonstrated natural aptitude for learning and enjoyed physical activities including traditional Bosnian dance.

While Amira thrived in many aspects of her early education, her first- and second-grade teachers had noted that she seemed to struggle with early reading skills despite her strong verbal abilities and conceptual understanding. Her parents had planned to seek additional support for these reading challenges just before the war erupted, disrupting all normal educational processes.

Displacement and Impact of War

The Bosnian War (1992–1995) erupted following the breakup of Yugoslavia, with Bosnia and Herzegovina declaring independence in 1992. What followed was a war characterized by widespread ethnic cleansing, systematic human rights abuses, and the siege of Sarajevo, the longest siege of a capital city in modern warfare, lasting nearly 4 years. An estimated 100,000 people died during the conflict, including approximately 40,000 Bosnian civilians. Over 2.2 million people were displaced, making it the most devastating conflict in Europe since World War II until the UN-protected safe area of Srebrenica fell in July 1995, resulting in the genocide of more than 8000 Bosnian men and boys.

This violent conflict dramatically disrupted Amira's education and development when she was 9 years old. As the siege of Sarajevo intensified, her family's neighborhood became increasingly dangerous, with regular shelling, snipers, and critical shortages of food, water, and electricity. Schools operated intermittently in basement shelters, with limited materials and constant security concerns. In this chaos, survival became the primary focus.

The trajectory of Amira's life changed dramatically during an artillery attack on their neighborhood. During the family's desperate attempt to reach a shelter, an explosion severely injured Amira. The blast resulted in traumatic injuries requiring amputation of her left leg below the knee and partial amputation of three fingers on her right hand. In the chaos of conflict and with limited medical infrastructure in besieged Sarajevo, her initial medical care was rudimentary, performed at a makeshift hospital with minimal resources, limited anesthesia, and few specialized surgical experts.

The specific nature of Amira's amputations created immediate and long-term physical challenges. The traumatic below-knee amputation of her left leg resulted in significant mobility limitations, requiring her to use crutches for all movement. Without proper rehabilitation or prosthetic services in the besieged city, the amputation site developed complications including uneven healing, persistent pain, and skin irritation from improper pressure distribution when using makeshift mobility aids. The partial amputation of three fingers on her right hand (index, middle, and ring fingers) created fine motor challenges that affected many daily activities, particularly those requiring precision grip or manipulation of small objects.

The cognitive and emotional impact of living under siege, combined with the trauma of her injuries, created additional challenges. Constant stress and trauma affected her concentration and adjustment to her new physical reality, while disrupted sleep and limited nutrition impacted her overall recovery and functioning. The educational environment during this period was entirely survival oriented, with no capacity to address her specific physical accommodation needs or previous reading challenges.

After nearly a year under siege, the family made the difficult decision to flee when a humanitarian corridor briefly opened. They left with only what they could carry, abandoning their home, most possessions, and the family's extensive library that had been a source of both professional resources and personal joy. This sudden departure severed Amira's connections to her extended family, her neighborhood community, and any educational continuity. The journey was particularly challenging for Amira, who had to navigate dangerous terrain with crutches and minimal support for her physical needs.

The family spent 18 months in a refugee camp in Croatia, where conditions were wholly inadequate for someone with Amira's physical needs. The camp environment presented numerous barriers: uneven ground that made crutch use difficult and dangerous, communal facilities without accessibility features, and limited privacy for managing hygiene and physical care. Educational opportunities were extremely limited, with makeshift schools operated by aid organizations focusing on basic literacy and numeracy with few resources for physical accommodations. In this setting, Amira's physical disabilities created significant barriers to accessing even this limited education.

Throughout this period, Amira's parents continued to support her learning and adjustment informally. They created exercises to develop her compensatory motor skills, maintained her educational development through verbal discussions and storytelling, and found creative ways to build her knowledge despite limited resources. Her father organized small discussion groups among camp children where Amira could participate without physical barriers. These adaptive approaches helped maintain her engagement with learning despite the challenging circumstances.

The family was eventually accepted into the United States' refugee resettlement program, based partly on their professional backgrounds, Amira's medical needs, and the educational needs of their children. The prospect of stable schooling, medical care, and potential support for Amira's physical rehabilitation needs was a significant factor in their decision to apply for resettlement in America rather than seeking to remain in Europe.

The Resettlement Journey to the United States

Arriving in Rochester, New York at age 12, Amira faced simultaneous challenges of cultural adaptation, language acquisition, and managing her physical disabilities in an entirely new environment. The United States offered her first access to comprehensive medical assessment and intervention for her amputations, nearly 3 years after her injuries. The initial medical evaluation documented significant complications from inadequate post-amputation care, leading to surgical revisions, intensive physical therapy, and the fitting of proper prosthetic devices.

Despite their educational credentials, Amira's parents initially found employment in service positions while working toward recertification. Language barriers complicated their ability to advocate effectively for Amira's physical accommodation needs during this early adjustment period. Rochester's small but established Bosnian Muslim community provided some cultural continuity and practical support during this transition, though within this community, there were often limited accommodations for physical disabilities in their mosques.

Initial Educational Placement and Identification of Multiple Disabilities

Amira's initial educational placement was based primarily on her age rather than her academic readiness, physical accommodation needs, or specific learning needs. Entering American schools with limited English proficiency and complex physical needs created a challenging situation. While her physical disabilities were immediately apparent, her teachers quickly noticed persistent difficulties with reading that seemed disproportionate to her otherwise rapid adaptation and strong verbal abilities.

Within 3 months of enrollment, Amira demonstrated impressive grasp of English conversational skills and actively participated in class discussions. Yet her reading fluency, decoding skills, and written work lagged significantly behind. Her teachers observed that she struggled with basic decoding, read laboriously, often missed small words, and avoided reading aloud. These challenges initially appeared consistent with normal second language acquisition, but her subject-area teachers noted that her reading difficulties seemed unusual compared to other ELL students with similar language exposure.

During a parent-teacher conference four months after her arrival, Amira's teachers shared these observations. Her parents revealed that before the war, Amira's teachers in Bosnia had identified similar reading struggles, and they had planned to seek additional support just before the conflict disrupted her education. This crucial information indicated her reading difficulties predated her trauma, displacement, and second language learning. Based on this revelation, the school promptly initiated a comprehensive special education evaluation to determine if she was eligible for services under the Individuals with Disabilities Education Act (IDEA).

Discovery of Dyslexia

As Amira settled into her American school experience and began making progress with her physical accommodations, her teachers quickly noticed persistent challenges with reading that seemed disproportionate to her otherwise quick adaptation. Initially, these difficulties were attributed to her English language learner (ELL) status, a common assumption for recently arrived refugee students.

During a parent-teacher conference just four months after her arrival, Amira's English and Social Studies teachers shared their observations about her reading difficulties. Rather than showing surprise, Amira's parents exchanged a meaningful glance before her mother explained, "In Bosnia, before the war, her teachers also mentioned she had troubles with reading. We thought perhaps she just needed more time, but then everything changed when the war came." During the displacement period, formal reading instruction was minimal, and her parents had focused primarily on keeping her connected to learning through oral storytelling and discussions.

This revelation provided crucial context for Amira's current struggles. Her reading difficulties were not solely attributable to English language acquisition but represented a pattern that predated her trauma, displacement, and second language learning. Her mother expressed both concern and relief: "We wondered if these problems would continue here, but with everything else, her leg, her hand, learning English, reading seemed less urgent. Perhaps now she can get the help she couldn't have during the war."

The school acted promptly upon this information. Within a week of the conference, Amira's case manager initiated a referral for a comprehensive special education evaluation to determine if she was eligible for special education services under IDEA. The school promptly sent Amira's parents a formal consent form explaining the evaluation process, which they signed and returned. This official consent started the legal timeline; the school district now had 60 calendar days to complete the evaluation and determine Amira's eligibility to determine whether her reading difficulties stemmed from a specific learning disability. The evaluation team carefully designed an assessment process that would:

1. Account for her multilingual background by incorporating assessment in both English and Bosnian where possible;

2. Distinguish between typical second language acquisition patterns and specific learning disabilities;

3. Consider the impacts of interrupted formal education during critical literacy development years;

4. Address the potential influences of trauma on learning and cognitive processing; and

5. Include culturally responsive components that would not disadvantage her based on cultural differences.

The evaluation process was completed efficiently within three weeks, well ahead of the mandated timeline. The comprehensive evaluation included standardized academic achievement testing with appropriate ELL accommodations, cognitive processing assessments focusing on phonological awareness and processing speed, reading assessments in both English and Bosnian (with a translator), classroom observations, work sample analysis, developmental history interviews, and vision and hearing screenings to rule out sensory factors. The team was careful to use evaluations that were culturally and linguistically appropriate, with nonverbal assessments when possible and consideration of Amira's interrupted formal education.

After gathering all assessment data, the evaluation team prepared written reports summarizing their findings. These reports documented Amira's strengths and challenges, detailed the assessment procedures used, explained test results in clear language, and included specific recommendations. Copies of these reports were provided to Amira's parents five days before the eligibility meeting, with a translator helping them understand the technical information.

The eligibility determination meeting included Amira's parents, the evaluation team members, her general education teachers, and a district representative who could commit resources. During this meeting, each specialist presented their findings and answered questions from Amira's parents. The data revealed a clear profile consistent with dyslexia. Amira showed significant weaknesses in phonological processing across both languages, difficulties with rapid automatic naming, inconsistent memory for visual-verbal associations, and reading fluency significantly below expected levels based on her cognitive abilities. Her pattern of errors was distinct from typical second language acquisition challenges.

The team systematically reviewed each of the IDEA eligibility criteria for specific learning disability:

1. Amira demonstrated a significant discrepancy between her intellectual ability and achievement in reading;
2. Her difficulties were not primarily the result of visual or hearing impairments, motor disabilities, or environmental factors;
3. She showed evidence of a processing disorder in the phonological component of language; and
4. She needed specialized instruction beyond what was available in the general education setting.

After reviewing all data, the team determined that Amira qualified for special education services under the specific learning disability category with dyslexia as the identified condition. This determination was documented on an eligibility form that all team members, including her parents, signed.

Once Amira was found eligible for special education services, the team had 30 days to develop her Individualized Education Program (IEP). The school scheduled an IEP meeting within 2 weeks, inviting Amira's parents, her general and special education teachers, related service providers, and an administrator who could allocate resources. Importantly, Amira herself was invited to participate in part of the meeting, as her involvement would foster self-advocacy skills.

Before the meeting, the special education teacher gathered input from all of Amira's teachers and drafted proposed goals based on her assessment results. At the IEP meeting, the team worked collaboratively to develop a comprehensive plan that addressed both her learning disability and physical needs. The IEP document comprehensively addressed Amira's educational needs through several key components. It began with Present Levels of Academic Achievement and Functional Performance that detailed her current reading, writing, and language skills alongside her physical functioning with prosthetics, documenting how both disabilities affected her classroom participation. The plan established measurable annual goals targeting specific literacy skills, such as improving her decoding accuracy of multisyllabic words from 45% to 85%. For services, Amira would receive 45 minutes of daily specialized reading instruction using an evidence-based dyslexia program, 30 minutes weekly of occupational therapy for hand-related writing challenges, and physical therapy consultation for accessibility issues. The IEP specified numerous accommodations including assistive technology, extended time, reduced copying requirements, and modified classroom furniture. It established that Amira would participate in regular state and district assessments with appropriate accommodations, and though not yet 16, included preliminary discussions about post-secondary transition planning to guide her future educational and vocational path.

Amira's parents actively participated in the IEP development process, providing input on goals and expressing concerns about balancing intensive intervention with inclusion in general education. The final IEP reflected a collaborative approach, with services carefully coordinated across providers.

At the conclusion of the meeting, her parents provided informed consent for the IEP to be implemented.

Once the IEP was finalized, implementation began immediately. The school designated a special education case manager who was responsible for communicating the IEP requirements to all of Amira's teachers, coordinating services, and monitoring her progress. The case manager also served as the primary contact for Amira's parents, providing regular updates on her progress and addressing any concerns.

The IEP included a specific schedule for progress monitoring, with data collection occurring every two weeks to track improvement toward her annual goals. The team committed to a formal review meeting after three months to evaluate the effectiveness of the interventions and make any necessary adjustments. Additionally, as required by IDEA, a complete annual review would be conducted within one year to reassess Amira's needs and update her IEP accordingly. A more comprehensive reevaluation would occur at least every three years to reassess her eligibility and needs.

By the end of her first semester in the United States, just five months after her arrival, Amira had a comprehensive IEP addressing both her physical needs and her dyslexia, developed through a legally sound process that ensured appropriate identification, parent participation, and targeted intervention. This prompt and thorough response demonstrated the school's commitment to meeting the complex educational needs of students with multiple disabilities.

Family Partnerships and Cultural Perspectives

Amira's parents remain her most consistent advocates, navigating complex American educational and medical systems while balancing their Bosnian Muslim cultural perspectives on disability. Their background as educators provides valuable insight but occasionally creates tension when American approaches differ from their experiences in Bosnia. They view her academic success not merely as individual achievement but as honoring their sacrifices and fulfilling the potential their flight from Bosnia was intended to preserve.

Communication between home and school initially presented challenges due to language differences and cultural frameworks for understanding disability. The school addressed these by connecting the family with a cultural liaison who bridged linguistic and cultural gaps. Regular home visits created opportunities for authentic communication in an environment where the family felt more comfortable expressing concerns. As trust developed, Amira's parents gradually took on more active roles in educational planning, eventually joining a parent advisory group for families of students with disabilities.

Questions for Teacher Educators

Contextual Analysis

1. How do the historical and sociopolitical circumstances of the Bosnian conflict shape Amira's understanding of her multiple disabilities, and what specific impacts might delayed intervention have had on her physical and literacy development?

2. What aspects of Bosnian Muslim cultural perspectives on disability might influence family approaches to supporting a child with both physical and learning disabilities?

3. How might Amira's experiences with physical and learning barriers inform her approach to navigating both environmental and cultural challenges in American schools?

4. What role does the family's background in education play in their current advocacy for Amira, and how might this professional knowledge influence their expectations of American schools?

5. How do the intersections of Amira's identities as a Muslim Bosnian refugee and a person with multiple disabilities create unique considerations for educational planning?

Physical Accessibility and Environmental Design

1. What specific environmental modifications would most significantly improve Amira's access to educational spaces and activities?

2. How can educators differentiate between challenges stemming from physical barriers, language acquisition, dyslexia, and educational gaps when assessing Amira's learning needs?

3. What approaches to physical education can ensure meaningful participation and physical development while accommodating limb differences?

4. How can classroom materials and activities be designed to accommodate both fine motor limitations and reading challenges without creating unnecessary attention to differences?

5. What transportation and mobility considerations should be addressed in planning field trips and extracurricular activities to ensure Amira's full participation?

Universal Design for Learning Implementation

1. How can curriculum materials be designed to provide multiple means of representation that accommodate physical access, language development, and reading challenges?

2. What approaches to group work and collaborative learning can ensure meaningful participation for students with both physical and learning disabilities?

3. How might digital tools be effectively implemented to support both physical access and literacy development without creating technology barriers?

4. What flexible assessment frameworks can accommodate physical limitations, developing English proficiency, and dyslexia while maintaining appropriate academic expectations?

5. How can classroom environments be designed to support physical access and effective learning through intentional space arrangement and materials selection that benefits students with multiple disabilities?

Cultural Integration and Identity Development

1. What structured approaches can help peers understand and respect both Amira's physical and learning needs and Muslim Bosnian background without creating uncomfortable focus on her differences?

2. How can educators support Amira in developing a positive identity that integrates her multiple disabilities, cultural heritage, and emerging understanding of American contexts?
3. What opportunities for leadership and contribution could highlight Amira's strengths while building social connections with peers?
4. How might educators address potential conflicts between cultural perspectives on disability and American educational approaches to independence and self-advocacy?
5. What strategies can help Amira maintain connection to her Bosnian Muslim cultural identity while adapting to American educational expectations around disability?

Family-School Partnerships

1. How can educators effectively communicate about multiple disabilities across language differences and potentially differing cultural understandings?
2. What approaches can honor the educational expertise of Amira's parents while providing information about interventions and accommodations that may not have been available in their home country?
3. How might schools adapt family engagement opportunities to be accessible to parents who may have limited English proficiency with medical and educational terminology while having strong general language skills?
4. What collaborative frameworks between medical providers, prosthetists, physical therapists, reading specialists, educators, and culturally informed staff can create integrated support systems rather than fragmented services?
5. How can schools support family members in maintaining their educational advocacy while navigating an unfamiliar disability accommodation system with terminology and procedures that differ significantly from their professional experience in Bosnia?

Literacy Development and Dyslexia Intervention

1. What evidence-based literacy interventions are most appropriate for adolescent English language learners with dyslexia?
2. How can educators effectively differentiate between reading challenges stemming from second language acquisition and those related to dyslexia?
3. What assistive technologies can support reading and writing for students with both fine motor limitations and dyslexia?
4. How can content-area teachers modify instruction and materials to support access to grade-level content while addressing reading challenges?
5. What approaches to teaching metacognitive strategies can help Amira develop independence in managing her reading challenges across different academic contexts?

References

Filipovic, Z. (1994). *Zlata's diary: A child's life in wartime Sarajevo.* Viking.

Hadzimuratovic, H. (2021). *My first trip to Bosnia & Herzegovina.* Independently published.

Maass, P. (1996). *Love thy neighbor: A story of war.* Vintage Books.

Nović, S. (2015). *Girl at war.* Random House.

Reid, A., & Schofield, H. (2011). *Goodbye Sarajevo: A true story of courage, love and survival.* Bloomsbury Publishing.

Sabic-El-Rayess, A., & Sullivan, S. (2020). *The cat I never named: A true story of love, war, and survival.* Bloomsbury Publishing.

Suljagic, E. (2005). *Postcards from the grave.* Saqi Books.

Trebincevic, K., & Shapiro, S. (2014). *The Bosnia list: A memoir of war, exile, and return.* Beacon Press.

CHAPTER TWO

Amir:

Understanding Neurodiversity and Creating Supportive Learning Environments for Students with Autism

Background

BORN WITHIN THE CONFINES of an immigration detention center, Amir's earliest experiences contrast sharply with typical childhood development. His parents, fleeing persecution in Myanmar, sought safety but instead found themselves indefinitely detained. The detention center, with its institutional setting, harsh lighting, constant noise, and overcrowded conditions, created a particularly challenging environment for Amir's early neurological development.

Birth and Early Development in Detention

From infancy, Amir displayed signs that would later be recognized as autism spectrum disorder. He showed intense discomfort with certain sensory inputs, particularly the frequent alarms and announcements over loudspeakers that characterized daily life in detention. He covered his ears and rocked persistently during these events. Unlike many children who sought physical comfort when distressed, Amir often withdrew from touch during these episodes, creating initial confusion for his parents who interpreted this as rejection rather than a sensory need.

The detention center environment itself exacerbated Amir's developmental challenges. Standard infant and toddler experiences that support neurological development such as exploring varied environments, encountering diverse sensory inputs, and interacting with a wide range of people were severely restricted. The limited physical space, monotonous setting, and absence of appropriate play materials limited opportunities for the kind of environmental stimulation that nurtures neural pathways during critical developmental periods.

The Burmese Government and Persecution of the Rohingya

The Rohingya, a Muslim minority group primarily residing in Myanmar's Rakhine State, have faced systematic discrimination for decades. The Myanmar government has refused to recognize Rohingya as citizens, effectively rendering them stateless through the 1982 citizenship law that excluded them from officially recognized ethnic groups.

This institutional discrimination has resulted in restrictions on freedom of movement, education, healthcare, and employment opportunities. The situation worsened in 2016–2017 when military operations forced hundreds of thousands of Rohingya to flee to Bangladesh.

For families like Amir's, these circumstances created an impossible situation that forced them to flee despite the risks involved in seeking asylum elsewhere. This context helps explain the intergenerational trauma affecting the Rohingya community, including children like Amir who, though born outside Myanmar, inherit the psychological impacts of their community's collective experiences.

Family Advocacy and Cultural Preservation

The Rohingya people, to whom Amir's family belongs, have a rich cultural heritage encompassing distinct linguistic, artistic, and religious practices. Their Islamic faith provides not merely a set of beliefs but an integral aspect of community identity, offering a moral framework and sense of collective belonging. For Amir, however, this cultural connection manifests differently than it would for a neurotypical child due to his concrete thinking and literal understanding of the world.

Amir's parents, particularly his mother Fatima, work diligently to maintain cultural connections despite their displacement, adapting traditional practices to accommodate Amir's autism. Understanding his difficulty with abstract concepts like "heritage" and "identity," Fatima focuses on concrete, tangible aspects of their culture: the precise movements of prayer five times daily, the exact recipes for traditional foods prepared with limited detention center ingredients, and the rhythmic patterns of Rohingya songs.

The detention center houses refugees from various countries and cultural backgrounds, creating a multilingual and multicultural environment.

While this diversity might enrich some children's cultural understanding, for Amir, the inconsistent language use and varying cultural expectations create additional confusion. His literal interpretation of language, characteristic of his autism, makes it particularly difficult to navigate this complex linguistic landscape. His parents serve as crucial cultural interpreters, explaining different behavioral expectations and social rules that Amir cannot intuitively understand.

Educational Experiences in Detention

The detention center's approach to neurodevelopmental conditions exposed a fundamental breakdown in institutional support. Medical documentation for children like Amir existed as fragmented, often mistranslated observations scattered across incomplete forms. No standardized protocol existed for sharing developmental information about children with neurodevelopmental conditions. Psychological assessments, when rarely conducted, were hurried and superficial, performed by overworked staff with minimal specialized training in autism spectrum disorders, particularly in the context of forced displacement.

The humanitarian system viewed Amir's needs through an administrative lens rather than a human one. Different departments such as medical, educational, and social services operated in isolation, creating invisible barriers that made comprehensive support almost impossible. Psychological assessments became bureaucratic exercises, reducing Amir's complex neurological experience to checkboxes and brief, interrupted consultations with limited translation.

This fragmented approach reflects the broader challenges in identifying and supporting refugees with disabilities documented in humanitarian research. As UNHCR guidance notes, "simply asking whether someone has a disability, with a yes/no response option, or identifying persons with disabilities based on visual cues, is not sufficient." The inadequate identification of Amir's autism exemplifies this problem, with his behavioral differences often attributed to trauma or cultural factors rather than recognized as a neurodevelopmental condition requiring specific supports.

Trauma and Its Intersection with Autism

While Amir was born in detention and has no direct memory of the violence his family fled, he carries the intergenerational trauma of his community and experiences ongoing traumatic stress from detention conditions. This trauma interacts with his autism in complex ways that require careful assessment and support.

Amir's parents, particularly his father Hassan, witnessed violence before fleeing Myanmar. Hassan experiences symptoms of PTSD including nightmares, flashbacks, and periods of emotional numbness that affect his ability to provide consistent support for Amir. While trying to protect Amir from knowledge of these experiences, Hassan's trauma responses create an unpredictable emotional environment that is particularly difficult for Amir to navigate given his need for emotional consistency.

The detention environment itself creates ongoing traumatic stress through environmental conditions that would be challenging for any child but are particularly difficult for a child with sensory sensitivities: overcrowded living spaces with minimal privacy, unpredictable regime changes, frequent security checks, and institutional routines that prioritize control over comfort. For children with autism, who typically require higher levels of predictability and control to feel safe, these circumstances create particularly acute stress responses.

Amir's specific trauma responses include sleep disturbances, increased stimming behaviors, selective mutism during periods of heightened stress, and occasional episodes of aggression when cornered or overwhelmed. Traditional trauma-informed approaches often rely on verbal processing and emotional expression that may be inaccessible to Amir given his communication profile. Similarly, typical autism interventions may not account for the impact of trauma on his regulatory systems and sense of safety. This intersection requires thoughtful integration of approaches that address both his neurological differences and traumatic experiences.

Social Relationships and Community Integration

Amir's social world is primarily defined by relationships within the detention center community, with his parents serving as essential advocates, interpreters, and buffers between him and an environment not designed for children with autism.

Within his family, Amir is deeply attached to his mother Fatima, who has become his primary advocate. Without formal understanding of autism, she has intuitively developed strategies that support his needs. She meticulously creates consistent routines within the constraints of detention, using hand-drawn visual schedules and predictable sequences to help Amir navigate daily activities. When detention center staff misinterpret Amir's behaviors as defiance, Fatima consistently intervenes, explaining his needs and negotiating accommodations.

His relationship with his father Hassan is more complex. Hassan struggles to understand Amir's literal interpretation of language and difficulty with emotional reciprocity, sometimes interpreting these as personal rejection. His own trauma responses manifest as irritability and withdrawal that Amir finds confusing, as he cannot intuitively understand the connection between past experiences and present emotions. Despite these challenges, Hassan has become Amir's fierce advocate with authorities, documenting how detention conditions worsen his son's autism symptoms and repeatedly requesting appropriate educational and medical supports through formal channels.

Peer relationships within the detention center have become increasingly difficult as Amir ages. Unlike neurotypical children who intuitively adapt to increasingly complex social rules, Amir continues to approach social interactions with the same direct strategies he used as a younger child. This growing gap between his social approach and peer expectations results in frequent misunderstandings and rejection. Some children actively exclude him, mock his stimming behaviors, or deliberately trigger sensory overload, having discovered they can provoke dramatic reactions by making sudden loud noises near him.

This social vulnerability reflects the heightened risk of bullying and abuse faced by children with disabilities in displacement settings. As UNHCR guidance notes, "children with disabilities are almost four times more likely to become victims of violence than are children without disabilities." For Amir, this vulnerability is compounded by the lack of structured social support programs or disability awareness within the detention environment.

Educational Gaps and Lost Opportunities

The educational provisions within the detention center are woefully inadequate for a child with Amir's specific learning needs. Classes are conducted in crowded rooms with minimal visual supports, constantly changing instructors, and curricula designed for neurotypical children. No individualized educational plan exists to address Amir's specific learning style, and teachers receive no training in supporting students with autism.

For Amir, who learns best through visual supports, concrete examples, and predictable routines, this educational environment creates almost insurmountable barriers. Despite his strong visual memory and aptitude for patterns, potential strengths that could support academic learning, he makes minimal educational progress in this setting. The constant environmental distractions, incomprehensible social demands, and lack of appropriate accommodations prevent him from demonstrating his actual capabilities.

This educational situation exemplifies the "lost generation" concern raised in humanitarian research, where children's education is profoundly disrupted by displacement. For children with disabilities like Amir, this disruption is compounded by the absence of specialized supports that might mitigate the impact of unstable educational environments. The resulting gaps in foundational skills and knowledge create long-term disadvantages that persist even if more appropriate educational settings become available in the future.

Preparing for Transition

As Amir approaches his 10th birthday, his family's case for asylum in Australia is under final review. This potential transition represents both hope for improved circumstances and significant challenges. While most children can adapt gradually to change, Amir's autism means transitions of any kind can trigger extreme distress without extensive preparation and support.

The uncertainty of their legal status creates ongoing stress that Amir experiences in fundamentally different ways than his family members. Immigration proceedings represent an abstract system that Amir cannot conceptualize. His inability to tolerate ambiguity is not defiance or impatience but a neurological need for concrete information that the asylum process simply cannot provide.

Recognizing this challenge, Amir's parents have developed creative strategies to make the potential transition more comprehensible to him. Fatima has created a visual calendar marking known appointments and using specific colors to indicate "waiting days," giving Amir a concrete way to understand the passage of time during this uncertain period.

Mental health professionals at the detention center have documented significant regression in Amir's functioning during previous relocations within the system. Even minor changes to housing units resulted in increased stereotypic behaviors, sleep disturbances, and periods of selective mutism lasting weeks. These documented patterns suggest that the upcoming transition, regardless of the outcome, will likely trigger similar or more severe regression without extraordinary support measures, support that detention facilities are typically ill-equipped to provide.

When detention center staff provide generic information about resettlement, Amir's parents must translate these abstract concepts into concrete terms he can understand. They have requested specific photographs of potential housing, schools, and community spaces in Australia to help Amir create a visual framework for the transition. Without such concrete preparation, even positive changes risk triggering severe regression in his functioning.

Resilience and Protective Factors

Despite the extraordinary challenges Amir faces, several key protective factors support his resilience. His parents' unwavering advocacy, particularly their persistent efforts to educate detention staff about his needs, has created small but meaningful accommodations that make his daily life more manageable. Their creative adaptations of limited materials to create visual supports, sensory tools, and predictable routines demonstrate remarkable resourcefulness in an environment designed for control rather than development.

Amir's own cognitive profile includes strengths that help him navigate his challenging environment. His exceptional memory for visual information and sequences allows him to predict and prepare for certain institutional routines. His intense interest in astronomy provides a cognitive escape from the limitations of detention, and his parents encourage this interest by gathering books, images, and information about space whenever possible.

A small but dedicated group of detention center staff have recognized Amir's unique needs and work within institutional constraints to provide additional support. A security officer who noticed Amir's distress during shift changes began giving him advance warning about personnel rotations. A volunteer teacher recognized his visual learning strength and created personalized picture cards to support his communication and learning.

The Rohingya community within the detention center provides another layer of support and protection. Community members share resources, create small celebrations of cultural traditions, and maintain linguistic connections that will be valuable if the family is eventually resettled in Australia.

They celebrate Ramadan, Eid, and other Islamic traditions that bring their families together. This community context offers Amir a sense of belonging and cultural continuity despite the institutional environment.

Future Possibilities and Concerns

As Amir's family awaits the outcome of their asylum application, multiple possible futures exist. If granted asylum in Australia, they will face the challenge of quickly establishing appropriate educational and therapeutic supports in a new community. Amir will need specialized assessment to determine appropriate educational placement and develop an intervention plan that addresses both his autism-related needs and the impacts of long-term detention on his development.

The family will need to navigate complex health and educational systems while still managing the practical challenges of resettlement: securing housing, establishing financial stability, and building community connections. For Amir's parents, this will mean balancing their own recovery from trauma and displacement with intensive advocacy for their son's specific needs in systems they are just beginning to understand.

If their asylum application is rejected, the family faces even greater challenges. Continued detention would likely cause further deterioration in Amir's functioning as he approaches adolescence in an environment unable to meet his developmental needs. The potential for return to Myanmar would place the family at risk while removing Amir from even the limited supports available in the detention environment.

These uncertainties underscore the profound vulnerability of refugee children with disabilities, whose developmental needs and potential are often overshadowed by legal and political considerations regarding migration and asylum. Amir's future depends not only on his family's remarkable resilience and advocacy but on systemic responses that recognize and address the specific needs of children at the intersection of displacement and disability.

Questions for Teacher Educators

Contextual Analysis

1. How does Amir's birth and development within a detention center shape his understanding of the world, and what specific impacts might

institutional environments have on sensory processing for children with autism?

2. What aspects of Rohingya cultural heritage might influence family perspectives on autism, and how might educators recognize and value family interpretations that differ from dominant Western medical models?
3. How might educators support Amir's family in maintaining cultural practices that provide predictability and comfort for him, even when Amir himself may not understand their abstract cultural significance?
4. What role can parents play as cultural interpreters between school systems and their children with autism, and how can educators validate and incorporate their expertise?
5. How do the sensory aspects of institutional environments specifically impact neurological development for children with autism, and what role can parents play in identifying effective environmental modifications?

Cognitive Safety and Learning Environment

1. What specific environmental modifications could create predictability and reduce sensory overwhelm for Amir in transition to a mainstream classroom setting?
2. How can educators differentiate between autism-related behaviors, trauma responses, and cultural adaptations when assessing Amir's learning needs?
3. What concrete strategies could support Amir's need for routine while gradually building flexibility and transition skills?
4. How might the physical organization of learning spaces address both sensory needs and psychological safety for students with similar profiles?
5. What approaches to instruction might accommodate Amir's literal language interpretation while supporting development of more flexible thinking?

Universal Design for Learning Implementation

1. How could multiple means of engagement be implemented to leverage Amir's intense interest in astronomy across different subject areas?

2. What alternative means of representation would accommodate both Amir's sensory processing differences and his cultural and linguistic background?

3. How could assessment methods be redesigned to provide Amir with multiple means of action and expression that accommodate his communication preferences?

4. What specific accommodations would support Amir during social learning activities that involve metaphorical language or require understanding of social nuances?

5. How might UDL principles be applied to create predictable routines and transitions that reduce Amir's anxiety and support his engagement?

Supporting Family Advocacy and Social Understanding

1. How can educators effectively partner with Amir's parents, recognizing them as experts on his specific needs and communication patterns rather than assuming professional knowledge supersedes their insights?

2. What structures and supports can schools provide to help Amir's parents prepare him for transitions and changes within the school environment?

3. How can educators help neurotypical peers understand Amir's autism-related differences without expecting him to demonstrate self-awareness or social understanding beyond his developmental capabilities?

4. What approaches can validate the expertise Amir's parents have developed through necessity, incorporating their successful strategies into classroom practices?

5. How might schools support family members in maintaining their advocacy energy while preventing burnout from constantly interpreting between their child and educational systems?

Trauma-Informed Practice Implementation

1. How do autism characteristics potentially amplify the impact of traumatic experiences, and what implications does this have for classroom practice?

2. What trauma-informed practices could help create a sense of safety and predictability for Amir without relying heavily on verbal processing?

3. How can educators distinguish between autism-related sensory reactions and trauma triggers in Amir's behavioral responses?

4. What approaches could help Amir develop emotional regulation skills that address both trauma responses and autism-related sensory overwhelm?

5. How might strengths-based approaches to learning simultaneously address trauma impacts and autism-related challenges?

References

Craig, D. (2018). *Finding home: A memoir about the Rohingya genocide.* Self-published.

Habiburahman & Ansel, S. (2019). *First, they erased our name: A Rohingya speaks.* Scribe Publications.

Ibrahim, A. (2018). *The Rohingya: Inside Myanmar's hidden genocide.* Oxford University Press.

Islam, M. N., Khan, M. S., & Bülbül, K. (Eds.). (2021). *Rohingya refugee crisis in Myanmar: Ethnic conflict and resolution.* Springer.

Wade, F. (2017). *Myanmar's enemy within: Buddhist violence and the making of a Muslim "other."* Zed Books.

Ware, A., & Laoutides, C. (2018). *Myanmar's 'Rohingya' conflict.* Hurst Publishers.

CHAPTER THREE

Zahra: Supporting Refugee Students with Traumatic Brain Injury in Inclusive Classrooms: Strategies for Accommodation and Empowerment

Background

FROM 1994 TO MID-JULY, the Rwandan genocide claimed approximately 800,000 to 1,000,000 lives in just 100 days, making it one of the most rapid mass killings in modern history. The violence erupted following decades of colonial-inflamed tensions between the Hutu majority and Tutsi minority, ultimately triggered by the assassination of Hutu President Juvénal Habyarimana on April 6, 1994. Hutu extremists orchestrated a systematic campaign that mobilized military forces, militias, and even ordinary citizens to target Tutsis and moderate Hutus through roadblocks, home invasions, and mass executions. Despite the scale and brutality of the violence, the international community largely failed to intervene, with the United Nations peacekeeping force in Rwanda severely under-resourced and restricted in its mandate. The genocide finally ended when the Tutsi-led Rwandan Patriotic Front (RPF) gained military control of the country, though the aftermath saw massive refugee crises, continued regional instability, and the monumental challenge of rebuilding a traumatized society.

Zahra, a 15-year-old Tutsi Rwandan refugee living in the United States, represents the complex intersection of traumatic brain injury, forced displacement, and educational adaptation. Her journey from conflict-affected western Rwanda to an American classroom illuminates both the significant challenges faced by students with cognitive disabilities in new cultural contexts and the remarkable resilience they can develop. Through Zahra's story, we explore how educators can implement strategies that address her cognitive needs while supporting her cultural transition and language development.

Early Life and Brain Injury in Rwanda

Born in western Rwanda, Zahra grew up in a Tutsi community with strong family connections. Her father worked as a teacher while her mother sold handcrafted baskets. Until age 11, Zahra developed typically, showing strong academic aptitude and enjoying traditional Rwandan dance and music.

This stability ended when ethnic tensions led to an attack on their village. During their escape, Zahra suffered a traumatic brain injury when a falling beam struck her head. In the chaos, she received only basic emergency medical attention. Her injury involved both focal damage to her left frontal lobe and diffuse axonal injury, primarily affecting cognitive functions rather than physical abilities. The impact manifested in deficits to memory, attention, processing speed, and executive functioning.

Without proper medical care, her family relied on traditional healing practices combined with limited modern medications. Her mother developed intuitive strategies to manage Zahra's confusion and memory challenges, including consistent routines and simple memory exercises.

Displacement and Refugee Camp Experiences

Escalating violence against Tutsi communities forced Zahra's family to flee western Rwanda, beginning a three-year displacement period. They initially stayed with relatives before seeking protection in a UNHCR refugee camp in Uganda. This transition was especially difficult for Zahra, whose brain injury made adapting to changing environments extremely challenging.

The refugee camp environment compounded her cognitive difficulties. Crowded conditions with constant noise exacerbated her attention problems and sensory sensitivities. Healthcare was minimal, with few professionals trained in brain injury rehabilitation. Educational opportunities were sporadic and not adapted for cognitive disabilities. In makeshift classrooms with large student numbers, Zahra's academic progress stalled as she struggled with memory and processing challenges.

Despite these limitations, Zahra's parents showed remarkable resourcefulness. Her father created memory exercises and adapted teaching approaches, while her mother maintained consistent routines beneficial for brain injury recovery. The family integrated traditional Rwandan healing approaches with the limited medical care available, incorporating prayers and ceremonies from community elders that provided psychological comfort and cultural continuity.

Educational Experiences in the United States

After three years in the refugee camp, Zahra's family was accepted into the U.S. refugee resettlement program. The resettlement process involved multiple screenings and transitions that were cognitively demanding for Zahra. Her parents used picture cards and familiar songs to help her manage the sensory overload of travel.

Upon arrival in Ann Arbor, Michigan, the family received support from a resettlement agency, but the orientation provided minimal information about special education services or brain injury resources. Limited English proficiency further complicated their ability to advocate for Zahra's needs.

At age 14, Zahra entered 8th grade based on her age rather than her academic readiness or English proficiency. The school initially focused almost exclusively on her status as an English Language Learner, overlooking her brain injury. Standard ESL methods, which relied on rapid information processing and quick responses, were precisely the areas affected by her injury. When she struggled, these difficulties were attributed to language barriers rather than neurological differences.

Classroom environments with high sensory stimulation, rapid transitions, and expectations for quick processing often triggered cognitive fatigue and emotional outbursts. Without understanding her brain injury, teachers sometimes misinterpreted these responses as behavioral issues.

The turning point came during a parent-teacher meeting with an interpreter, where Zahra's parents revealed her traumatic brain injury. This crucial information had not been previously documented in her educational records. With this new understanding, school officials recognized that her challenges stemmed from more than just language acquisition issues.

Special Education Eligibility and Legal Framework

Following the identification of Zahra's traumatic brain injury, the school district conducted a comprehensive evaluation to determine her eligibility for special education services under the Individuals with Disabilities Education Act (IDEA). This federal law ensures that students with disabilities who require specialized instruction receive appropriate educational services and supports.

Zahra qualified for special education under the IDEA category of "traumatic brain injury" (TBI), which is defined as "an acquired injury to the brain caused by an external physical force, resulting in total or partial functional disability or psychosocial impairment, or both, that adversely affects a child's educational performance" 34 C.F.R. § 300.8(c)(12) (2006). The documentation of her injury from the falling beam during her family's escape from Rwanda, combined with the observable impact on her cognitive functioning, clearly established her eligibility under this category.

The evaluation team gathered evidence demonstrating how Zahra's traumatic brain injury adversely affected her educational performance in several key areas:

1. **Memory deficits:** Difficulty retaining new information, particularly when presented verbally without visual supports

2. **Attention regulation:** Challenges maintaining focus in stimulating environments and difficulty shifting attention between tasks

3. **Processing speed:** Significant delays in processing verbal information, especially complex or multi-step instructions

4. **Executive functioning:** Struggles with organization, planning, task initiation, and completion of multi-stage assignments

5. **Cognitive fatigue:** Decreased performance and increased emotional reactivity after sustained mental effort

The evaluation process was carefully designed to distinguish between challenges stemming from her traumatic brain injury and those related to language acquisition or cultural adjustment. Assessment tools were selected that minimized cultural and linguistic bias, and the evaluation team included professionals with expertise in both traumatic brain injury and English language acquisition. A cultural liaison helped interpret assessment results within the context of Rwandan educational expectations and cultural perspectives on learning.

The determination of eligibility recognized that Zahra requires specially designed instruction that goes beyond typical English Language Learner supports or general classroom accommodations. Her IEP was developed to address both her neurological needs and language acquisition goals through an integrated approach that acknowledges how these areas interact rather than addressing them as separate concerns.

This legal framework ensures that Zahra receives appropriate educational services, procedural safeguards, and regular progress monitoring to support her academic success. It provides her family with meaningful participation in educational decision-making and establishes their right to due process if disagreements arise regarding her educational program.

Cognitive Accommodations and Educational Strategies

Following this comprehensive evaluation process, Zahra's educational team has developed specific classroom strategies to address the cognitive processing challenges resulting from her traumatic brain injury. These strategies focus on three primary areas of impact: attention regulation, information processing, and executive functioning.

To support attention regulation, teachers implement environmental modifications that minimize distractions and sensory overload. Zahra's seating is positioned away from high-traffic areas and windows, reducing visual distractions that compete for attention. Classes with naturally higher noise levels or sensory stimulation (like physical education, music, or crowded hallways during transitions) now include designated "regulatory pauses" where she can take a brief sensory break with noise-canceling headphones before sensory overload triggers cognitive fatigue or emotional responses.

For information processing challenges, teachers adjust their instructional approach in several ways. They provide written or visual supplements to verbal instructions, allowing Zahra to reference information that might otherwise be lost due to processing speed differences. Complex information is chunked into smaller units with processing time built in between segments. When introducing new concepts, teachers explicitly connect to previously mastered information, supporting her ability to build coherent knowledge structures despite memory challenges. A note-taking partner system provides backup for information she might miss during lectures, allowing her to focus on understanding rather than documenting content.

Executive functioning supports address her challenges with organization, prioritization, and task initiation. These include consistent routines at the beginning and end of each class period, explicit step-by-step procedures for multi-stage assignments, and task checklists for longer projects. Teachers check comprehension of instructions privately rather than calling on her in front of the class, reducing anxiety that can further impair executive function. Digital organizational tools help compensate for memory challenges through reminders, calendars, and assignment tracking systems that reduce cognitive load.

In addition to these classroom strategies, Zahra receives two 30-minute sessions weekly with a speech-language pathologist who specializes in cognitive-communication disorders. These sessions focus on developing metacognitive strategies that help her recognize when she's missed information, identify situations likely to trigger cognitive overload, and implement self-advocacy approaches appropriate to different contexts. This specialized support helps bridge the gap between classroom accommodations and her developing self-management skills.

Zahra's educational team recognizes that her brain injury affects not just academic performance but energy management throughout the school day. Her schedule includes a daily "cognitive rest" period in a quiet environment, allowing her to manage fatigue that compounds academic challenges when not addressed. This proactive approach to energy management has reduced the frequency of overload episodes and improved her ability to engage consistently throughout the day.

Family Partnerships and Cultural Perspectives

Zahra's parents remain her most consistent advocates and support system, navigating complex American educational and medical systems while adapting their understanding of her needs across cultural frameworks. They approach her brain injury from a perspective that integrates traditional Rwandan understanding of health with the Western medical information they have received since resettlement.

The family's approach to Zahra's support reflects Rwandan cultural values emphasizing community interdependence rather than the individual independence often prioritized in American disability services. They view her success as a shared family responsibility rather than focusing primarily on developing her autonomy. This perspective sometimes creates tension with American educational approaches that emphasize independent functioning as a primary goal.

Communication between home and school presents ongoing challenges due to both language differences and cultural frameworks for understanding disability and education. While the school provides interpreters for formal meetings, daily communication often relies on Zahra's emerging English skills or simplified exchanges that may not fully capture important nuances. Cultural differences in directness of communication, appropriate advocacy approaches, and expectations around parent involvement create additional complications in building effective partnerships.

As trust developed between the family and school, Zahra's parents gradually took on more active roles in educational planning. They began attending school events more frequently, participated in a parent advisory group for families of students with disabilities, and eventually shared aspects of Rwandan culture through a community education event. These engagement opportunities helped shift the relationship from one-directional support to a more collaborative partnership that recognized their expertise and cultural knowledge.

Physical and Emotional Health Integration

Beyond cognitive supports, Zahra's team recognizes the essential interconnection between physical health, emotional well-being, and cognitive functioning for someone with traumatic brain injury. Her headaches, which occur with some regularity and significantly impact cognitive function, require coordinated management between school health services, medical providers, and family approaches. A protocol developed collaboratively with her neurologist allows the school nurse to provide appropriate medication and a quiet rest period when headaches emerge during the school day, preventing escalation that might otherwise result in missed instruction.

Sleep disruption, a common issue after traumatic brain injury, significantly impacts Zahra's cognitive function and emotional regulation. Addressing this has required both medical intervention through her primary care provider and practical family strategies to establish consistent sleep routines. The educational team accommodates occasional days with reduced function when sleep has been poor, recognizing the futility of pushing academic demands during these periods and instead focusing on maintenance activities that prevent regression but don't require optimal cognitive performance.

Emotional regulation challenges, which manifest as occasional tearfulness, frustration, or withdrawal when Zahra becomes overwhelmed, are approached through a trauma-informed lens that recognizes the interaction between her brain injury, displacement experiences, and adolescent development. A school counselor with expertise in both refugee adjustment and neurological impacts provides weekly sessions focused on developing emotional recognition and regulation strategies specific to her needs.

The occupational therapist on Zahra's team addresses the sensory sensitivity aspects of her brain injury, which include heightened reactions to fluorescent lighting, certain sound frequencies common in school environments, and tactile defensiveness that affects her comfort in typical classroom seating. Sensory accommodations including noise-reducing headphones, lighting modifications, and alternative seating options have significantly reduced the cognitive energy Zahra expends managing sensory input, allowing more resources for academic engagement.

Physical activity plays an important role in Zahra's overall management plan, as appropriate exercise has been shown to support cognitive function and emotional regulation after brain injury. The adaptive physical education teacher has developed a modified program that provides cardiovascular benefit without triggering headaches or excessive fatigue. This program incorporates elements of traditional Rwandan dance that provide both cultural connection and physical benefits without the competitive aspects of typical physical education that created anxiety and avoidance.

Educational Implications

For classroom teachers, Zahra's story emphasizes that invisible disabilities like traumatic brain injury may go unrecognized when other factors such as language acquisition or cultural adjustment seem to explain learning challenges. Careful observation and assessment are essential to distinguish cognitive processing differences from other learning barriers and provide appropriate support.

School systems must examine how typical instructional approaches in both language acquisition and special education programs may create barriers for students with multiple intersecting needs. Fast-paced instruction, heavy working memory demands, and limited processing time disadvantage students with traumatic brain injury; cultural misunderstandings about disability can further complicate appropriate service delivery. Integrated approaches that address cognitive needs while supporting language development and cultural transition create more effective learning environments.

For professional development, Zahra's case highlights the importance of collaboration across specialties often separated in school structures. When language acquisition specialists, special educators, cultural liaisons, and medical professionals coordinate their approaches, students with complex needs receive coherent support rather than fragmented interventions that may conflict or create unnecessary complexity. This collaboration requires intentional planning, regular communication channels, and mutual respect for different areas of expertise.

The timing and nature of accommodations becomes particularly important for students with traumatic brain injury and cultural transition. Initial supports should address immediate barriers to participation while more comprehensive evaluation provides deeper understanding of needs. Accommodations should evolve as students develop new skills, language proficiency increases, and the impacts of brain injury change through recovery and development. This dynamic approach requires ongoing assessment and flexibility rather than static support plans.

Ultimately, Zahra's journey challenges educators to move beyond single-category support models toward more holistic approaches that recognize the complex interplay between neurological differences, language acquisition, cultural transition, and identity development. By understanding these intersections and implementing thoughtful, culturally responsive accommodations, educators can unlock the potential of students navigating the complex terrain of brain injury and displacement.

Questions for Teacher Educators

Contextual Analysis

1. How do the historical and socioeconomic circumstances of Rwanda's ethnic conflicts shape Zahra's understanding of her brain injury, and

what specific impacts might limited healthcare access have had on her neurological recovery?

2. What aspects of Rwandan cultural perspectives on health and healing might influence family approaches to brain injury rehabilitation and cognitive support?

3. How might Zahra's experiences with cognitive challenges following her injury inform her approach to navigating both cognitive and cultural barriers in American schools?

4. What role does Zahra's refugee journey play in her current educational experience, and how might the physical and emotional challenges of displacement affect brain injury recovery?

5. How do the intersections of Zahra's identities as a Tutsi Rwandan refugee and a person with traumatic brain injury create unique considerations for educational planning?

Cognitive Access and Learning

1. What specific accommodations can effectively address cognitive processing needs while supporting language acquisition rather than treating them as separate issues?

2. How can educators differentiate between challenges stemming from brain injury, language barriers, and content knowledge when assessing Zahra's learning needs?

3. What strategies can support working memory and attention regulation while building academic language proficiency?

4. How can classroom activities be structured to accommodate processing speed differences without creating stigma or unnecessary separation from peers?

5. What approaches to homework and assessment can account for cognitive fatigue while maintaining appropriate academic expectations?

Universal Design for Learning Implementation

1. How can curriculum materials be designed to provide multiple means of representation that accommodate both cognitive processing needs and language development?

2. What approaches to group work and collaborative learning can ensure meaningful participation for students with processing speed and working memory challenges?

3. How might digital tools be effectively implemented to support both cognitive organization and language development without creating technology barriers?

4. What flexible assessment frameworks can accommodate fluctuating cognitive energy while maintaining appropriate academic expectations?

5. How can classroom environments be designed to minimize cognitive overload through intentional management of sensory input and information presentation?

Cultural Integration and Identity Development

1. What structured approaches can help peers understand and respect both Zahra's cognitive needs and cultural background without creating uncomfortable focus on her differences?

2. How can educators support Zahra in developing a positive identity that integrates her brain injury, cultural heritage, and emerging understanding of American contexts?

3. What opportunities for leadership and contribution could highlight Zahra's strengths while building social connections with peers?

4. How might educators address potential conflicts between cultural perspectives on disability and Western educational approaches to cognitive support?

5. What strategies can help Zahra maintain connection to her Rwandan cultural identity while adapting to American educational expectations?

Family-School Partnerships

1. How can educators effectively communicate about traumatic brain injury across language differences and potentially differing cultural understandings of cognitive disability?

2. What approaches can honor family expertise while providing information about educational options and cognitive support that may not have been available in their home country?

3. How might schools adapt family engagement opportunities to be accessible to relatives who may have limited English proficiency, work constraints, and unfamiliarity with American special education systems?

4. What collaborative frameworks between language specialists, special educators, and culturally informed staff can create integrated support systems rather than fragmented services?

5. How can schools support the development of self-advocacy skills while respecting cultural values that may emphasize community interdependence over individual autonomy?

References

Berry, M. E. (2018). *War, women, and power: From violence to mobilization in Rwanda and Bosnia-Herzegovina.* Cambridge University Press.

Benaron, N. (2012). *Running the rift: A novel.* Algonquin Books.

Faye, G. (2018). *Small country: A novel* (S. Ardizzone, Trans.). Hogarth. (Original work published as *Petit pays*)

Gourevitch, P. (1998). *We wish to inform you that tomorrow we will be killed with our families: Stories from Rwanda.* Farrar, Straus and Giroux.

Ilibagiza, I. (2006). *Left to tell: Discovering God amidst the Rwandan holocaust.* Hay House.

McDoom, O. S. (2021). *The path to genocide in Rwanda: Security, opportunity, and authority in an ethnocratic state.* Cambridge University Press.

Straus, S., & Waldorf, L. (Eds.). (2011). *Remaking Rwanda: State building and human rights after mass violence.* University of Wisconsin Press.

Wamariya, C., & Weil, E. (2018). *The girl who smiled beads: A story of war and what comes after.* Crown Publishing Group.

CHAPTER FOUR

Noor:

Finding Expression and Supporting Students with Selective Mutism and Communication Differences

Background

NOOR IS A 14-YEAR-OLD Iraqi girl who has known war and displacement for most of her life. Born and raised in a close-knit neighborhood in Baghdad, her childhood was shattered when the U.S. invasion of Iraq began in 2003. Noor was just 6 years old when the "Shock and Awe" bombing campaign rained devastation on her city, forever altering her family's existence. In the chaos and violence of the invasion, Noor's family lost everything. Their home was destroyed in a bombing raid, and in the panic to escape the falling debris, Noor became separated from her parents and siblings. She was found hours later, alone and in shock, by neighbors who took her in. It was only after several agonizing days that Noor was reunited with her family, who had desperately searched for her amidst the rubble and confusion. But their reunion was tainted by grief. Noor's younger brother had been killed when their house was hit. This devastating loss, coupled with the trauma of the invasion itself, marked a profound turning point for Noor and her family.

Life in the Refugee Camp

With their home destroyed and the city increasingly dangerous, Noor's family made the wrenching decision to seek safety elsewhere. They joined the tide of refugees fleeing the war-torn capital, eventually finding their way to a crowded refugee camp in Jordan. Life in the camp was a stark contrast to the warmth and stability of their former community in Baghdad. Noor's father, a respected schoolteacher, now struggled to find work to support the family. Her mother, once a lively presence always ready with a song or story, now moved through the days in a grief-stricken haze, the loss of her son an ever-present ache. It was here, in the bleak confines of the refugee camp, that Noor's voice began to fade away. The once talkative, expressive child grew increasingly silent in the aftermath of the traumas she had witnessed. At first, her family thought it was a temporary response to the shock of their uprooting. But as weeks stretched into months and Noor's silence grew more entrenched, it became clear that this was more than a passing phase. Selective mutism, a complex childhood anxiety disorder characterized by a persistent inability to speak in certain social situations, had taken hold. For Noor, the trauma of the war, the loss of her brother, and the displacement from her homeland had triggered a profound retreat inward. Speaking became associated with the unspeakable. To use her voice meant to confront the pain and terror of all she had endured.

In her new school within the refugee camp, Noor's silence was often misinterpreted as defiance or disengagement. Teachers, already overburdened and under-resourced, struggled to understand and accommodate her unique needs. Noor's academic potential was obscured by her inability to participate verbally, leading to frustration on all sides. Some classmates mocked or excluded her due to her silence, while others simply attributed her behavior to shyness. Fortunately, Noor found a small circle of friends who appreciated her for who she was and provided crucial emotional support. Despite the challenges, glimmers of hope and self-expression began to emerge for Noor. The school's modest library became a sanctuary where she could lose herself for hours in books, particularly volumes of Arabic poetry and illustrated folk tales. The librarian, noticing Noor's keen interest, began setting aside new arrivals for her and engaging her in written conversations about her favorite stories and verses. Noor's involvement in the school's drama club also provided an outlet for her to explore her creativity and express herself through movement and art, even if she remained silent.

Trauma-Informed Strategies for Classroom Participation

A compassionate teacher recognized Noor's potential and worked to create a more inclusive classroom environment. Visual cues and written instructions were used more frequently to support Noor's learning. She was given opportunities to demonstrate her understanding through drawings and written work rather than being forced to speak. The teacher took the time to educate her colleagues about selective mutism, fostering greater empathy and reducing misunderstandings. These accommodations, while not perfect, made a significant difference in Noor's school experience. At home, Noor's family grappled with their own grief while learning to support their daughter in new ways. Steeped in a cultural context where verbal expression and storytelling were highly valued, they initially struggled to understand and adapt to Noor's silence. At times, they wrestled with feelings of helplessness or worry that they had somehow failed their child. But they also drew upon deep wells of love and patience. Noor's father began sitting with her for hours, quietly observing as she pursued her interests. Her mother left small gifts on her pillow each morning, an unspoken gesture of support. And her younger sister became a fierce advocate, patiently interpreting Noor's wants and needs to the world.

As time passed, Noor found additional ways to express herself and process her experiences. She discovered a talent for vivid, expressive drawing and began filling notebooks with sketches that communicated her inner world. In the camp's art therapy sessions, Noor's gift for visual storytelling became increasingly apparent. Through her artwork, she could share her emotions, dreams, and memories without needing to utter a word. Noor's journey is far from over, and her path forward remains uncertain. The traumas of her past and the challenges of her present continue to shape her daily life in profound ways. But in the face of unthinkable adversity, Noor and her family have shown remarkable resilience. Through the support of loved ones, the understanding of key educators, and her own unwavering spirit, Noor continues to grow and find her voice, even if it takes a different form than most. Her story is a testament to the power of human connection, the importance of inclusive education, and the boundless potential of every child to learn, heal, and thrive when given the opportunity.

Resettlement in the United States

After several years in the refugee camp in Jordan, Noor's family was finally granted resettlement in the United States through the United Nations High Commissioner for Refugees (UNHCR) resettlement program. The news came after a lengthy and anxiety-filled application process, involving multiple interviews, health screenings, and background checks that spanned more than 2 years. When they finally received approval, the family experienced a complex mix of emotions: relief at leaving the limbo of camp life, hope for new opportunities, but also apprehension about starting over yet again in an unfamiliar culture.

The International Rescue Committee (IRC) sponsored their resettlement to a mid-sized city in the Midwest with an established Arab American community. In the weeks before departure, Noor's family attended cultural orientation sessions where they received basic information about American life, from using public transportation to understanding the education system. Nevertheless, nothing could fully prepare them for the reality of their new lives.

Upon arrival in the United States, the family was initially housed in a small, sparsely furnished two-bedroom apartment in a neighborhood with other immigrant families. The IRC caseworker helped them navigate immediate challenges: enrolling in government assistance programs, obtaining Social Security cards, scheduling health appointments, and connecting with local community resources. For the first 3 months, they received a modest stipend to cover basic expenses while they worked to establish themselves.

The resettlement process was both exciting and daunting, as they navigated a new set of cultural norms and expectations. Everyday tasks that had once been routine now required significant effort. Grocery shopping meant confronting unfamiliar food options and packaging. Paying bills introduced them to American banking systems. Even taking the bus required learning new routes and schedules. The language barrier compounded these challenges, particularly for Noor's mother, who had the least English proficiency in the family.

The family also had to adjust to a different pace of life and social dynamics. The closely-knit communal living they had known, both in Baghdad and later in the refugee camp, gave way to the more private, individualistic nature of American suburban life. Neighbors were polite but often distant, a stark contrast to the interdependent relationships they had relied upon previously. This social isolation was particularly difficult during religious holidays and family milestones, times when cultural traditions had always been shared communally.

Transition to American Schools

The transition to an American classroom brought new challenges for Noor. While her English had improved during her time in the camp, she still struggled with the academic language and fast-paced verbal interactions of her new school. Her selective mutism, which had started to improve slightly in the familiar surroundings of the camp, resurged in this new, unfamiliar environment.

Noor's teachers, unfamiliar with her background and the complexity of selective mutism, initially mistook her silence for a lack of understanding or engagement. They would often call on her in class, putting her on the spot and inadvertently increasing her anxiety. Some classmates, not understanding her condition, would tease her or exclude her from group activities.

After several weeks of observing Noor's difficulties, the school's ESL coordinator, who had experience working with refugee students, recognized that Noor might need additional support beyond the standard ESL accommodations. She noticed that Noor's selective mutism was significantly impacting her ability to participate in class and demonstrate her knowledge, despite her evident comprehension and engagement with written materials.

Special Education Referral Process

The ESL coordinator initiated a conversation with Noor's parents about the possibility of special education services. This was a challenging discussion, as Noor's parents came from a cultural context where special education carried different implications and stigmas. With the help of an Arabic interpreter, the coordinator explained that in the American education system, special education was designed to provide targeted support to help students overcome specific barriers to learning.

After obtaining parental consent, the school began the formal process to determine Noor's eligibility for special education services under the Individuals with Disabilities Education Act (IDEA). This started with a formal request for evaluation, which Noor's father signed after a meeting with the school counselor who carefully explained the purpose and process.

Comprehensive Evaluation and Assessment

The comprehensive evaluation process was thorough and multifaceted. It included educational assessments that examined Noor's academic skills through written and nonverbal tasks, alongside psychological evaluations that assessed the impact of her selective mutism and trauma on her learning. The school psychologist conducted observations of Noor in different school settings, while also reviewing her previous school records from the refugee camp. The team interviewed her parents about her developmental history and current functioning and conducted speech and language assessments to distinguish between selective mutism, ESL needs, and other potential communication disorders.

Throughout the evaluation process, the school team was careful to use culturally appropriate assessment tools and techniques, recognizing that standard evaluations might not accurately reflect Noor's abilities due to cultural and linguistic differences. They ensured that assessments were conducted in both English and Arabic when possible and that nonverbal components were emphasized.

Eligibility Determination

After the evaluation was complete, the school team, including the ESL coordinator, school psychologist, special education teacher, speech and language pathologist, and Noor's homeroom teacher, met with her parents to review the results. With the help of an interpreter, they determined that Noor met the eligibility criteria for special education services under two classifications: Emotional Disturbance, due to the impact of her trauma and selective mutism on her educational performance, particularly her ability to build and maintain relationships and express herself verbally in educational settings; and Other Health Impairment, related to her anxiety, which significantly limited her alertness to the educational environment by heightening her stress response in verbal communication situations.

The team carefully explained to Noor's parents that these classifications were not labels or diagnoses, but rather categories that would allow Noor to access appropriate educational supports. They emphasized that special education was individualized and focused on helping students succeed despite challenges.

Individualized Education Program Development

With Noor's eligibility established, the team worked collaboratively with her parents to develop an Individualized Education Program (IEP). This legal document outlined Noor's present levels of academic achievement and functional performance, measurable annual goals related to both her academic progress and communication development, the specific special education services and accommodations she would receive, how her progress would be measured and reported to her parents, and transition planning to help her develop independence and prepare for post-secondary options.

Noor's IEP included several key services and accommodations tailored to her unique needs. She would receive weekly sessions with a speech and language pathologist who specialized in selective mutism and regular meetings with a school counselor trained in trauma-informed approaches. Her teachers implemented a communication plan that allowed for alternative forms of class participation and provided extended time for assignments and assessments. When speaking in class was too difficult, Noor had permission to submit voice recordings made in private. The team incorporated gradual exposure therapy to help her become more comfortable with verbal communication over time, while also providing a visual communication system for situations when verbal communication was too challenging. Importantly, Noor was assigned a designated "safe person" at school whom she could seek out during times of high anxiety.

The IEP team was careful to balance high expectations for Noor's academic achievement with realistic goals for her communication development. They recognized that recovery from selective mutism would be a gradual process, especially given her trauma history, but they were committed to helping her make progress while providing appropriate accommodations.

Implementation of Special Education Services

With the IEP in place, Noor's teachers received training on how to support her unique needs while maintaining academic rigor. Visual supports, written instructions, and opportunities for nonverbal participation were incorporated into lessons. Noor was given the option to present assignments in alternative formats, such as through artwork or written pieces. Her teachers learned to give her space and not force verbal participation, while still engaging her through other means.

The special education case manager coordinated regular communication between all team members, ensuring that everyone working with Noor was consistent in their approach. Quarterly IEP meetings allowed the team to assess her progress and make adjustments as needed.

For Noor, the special education services provided a framework of support that acknowledged her unique challenges while recognizing her potential. While the journey was still difficult, having a formalized plan and a dedicated team made a significant difference in her educational experience and gradual communication development.

Family Dynamics and Cultural Adjustment

Noor's family also faced significant adjustments during the resettlement process. Her father, once a respected teacher, struggled to find work in his field due to language barriers and the challenges of credential transfer. He eventually found a job as a school janitor, a significant shift in status that weighed on him. Noor's mother, while relieved to be out of the camp, mourned the loss of their extended family and community support.

In their new urban apartment, the family felt isolated from the tight-knit community they had known in Baghdad and the shared experience of displacement in the refugee camp. They struggled to navigate American systems and cultural norms, often feeling lost and overwhelmed.

However, they also found strengths in their family bond and their faith. They connected with a local mosque, finding solace in familiar religious practices and gradually building new community connections. Noor's father, drawing on his teaching background, became a vocal advocate for his children's education. He regularly met with Noor's teachers and the special education team, bridging cultural gaps and ensuring that her needs were understood.

At home, the family worked to create a sense of safety and predictability for Noor. They maintained familiar routines and traditions, cooking favorite meals and celebrating important holidays. They also learned to communicate with Noor in new ways, using more nonverbal cues and respecting her silence while still encouraging her self-expression through art and writing.

Reflections for Educators

Noor's story illuminates the complex interplay of trauma, displacement, cultural identity, and communication in the lives of refugee students. It underscores the critical role that educators can play in creating safe, inclusive spaces where these students can learn, heal, and thrive.

Some key takeaways for educators include:

1. Trauma-informed care must be at the heart of working with refugee students. This means understanding the impacts of trauma on learning and behavior and creating predictable, safe classroom environments.

2. Communication comes in many forms. For students with selective mutism or language barriers, it's crucial to provide alternative ways to participate and demonstrate learning.

3. Cultural competence and partnership with families are essential. Understanding a student's cultural background and working closely with their family can provide invaluable insights and support.

4. Special education frameworks can provide crucial support when properly implemented with cultural sensitivity. The evaluation process must account for cultural and linguistic differences.

5. Patience and persistence are key. Students like Noor may take time to open up and progress may be incremental. Celebrating small victories and maintaining consistent support are crucial.

6. Refugee students have unique strengths and perspectives to share. By creating spaces where they can express themselves and feel valued, educators can help these students thrive and enrich the entire school community.

Ultimately, Noor's story is one of hope and resilience in the face of incredible adversity. It's a reminder of the transformative power of education when it is inclusive, trauma-informed, culturally responsive, and supported by appropriate special education services. As educators, we have the privilege and responsibility to help write the next chapters in stories like Noor's, supporting these remarkable students as they find their voices and their place in the world.

Questions for Teacher Educators

Contextual Analysis

1. How do the experiences of war and displacement in Iraq shape Noor's understanding of communication and emotional expression?

2. What specific impacts do prolonged exposure to conflict and loss have on a child's communication development and selective mutism?
3. How do the cultural and familial contexts of Iraqi refugee communities influence approaches to trauma, silence, and healing?
4. What role do community support systems play in supporting children experiencing communication differences in the aftermath of war?
5. How do the intersections of Noor's identities as an Iraqi refugee, a survivor of war trauma, and a young woman with selective mutism create unique considerations for educational support?

Cognitive Access and Communication

1. What alternative communication strategies can effectively support students with selective mutism while honoring their emotional and cultural experiences?
2. How can educators differentiate between communication challenges stemming from trauma, cultural adjustment, and individual communication differences?
3. What approaches can support emotional expression and communication development for students who have experienced severe psychological trauma?
4. How can classroom activities be structured to create safe, supportive environments for students struggling with verbal communication?
5. What assessment methods can accurately capture the academic potential of students who cannot or choose not to communicate verbally?

Universal Design for Learning Implementation

1. How can curriculum materials be designed to provide multiple means of expression that accommodate students with communication differences?
2. What approaches to learning can create meaningful participation opportunities for students with selective mutism?

3. How might arts-based and nonverbal communication tools be effectively integrated into classroom learning?

4. What flexible assessment frameworks can accommodate students' varied communication abilities while maintaining academic rigor?

5. How can classroom environments be designed to minimize anxiety and support gradual communication development?

Cultural Integration and Identity Development

1. What strategies can help students like Noor maintain connection to their cultural identity while adapting to new educational environments?

2. How can educators support the development of a positive identity that integrates experiences of trauma, displacement, and communication differences?

3. What opportunities for leadership and contribution could highlight the strengths of students with selective mutism?

4. How might schools address potential conflicts between cultural perspectives on communication and verbal expression?

5. What approaches can help peers understand and respect students' communication differences without creating additional stigma?

Family-School Partnerships

1. How can educators effectively communicate with families about communication differences and special education services across language and cultural barriers?

2. What approaches can honor family expertise and cultural understanding while providing support for students with selective mutism?

3. How might schools adapt family engagement opportunities to be accessible to refugee families with complex backgrounds?

4. What collaborative frameworks can create integrated support systems that address both educational and emotional needs?

5. How can schools support the development of communication skills while respecting cultural values and individual healing processes?

Community-Engaged Learning Opportunities

1. Develop multilingual communication workshops that explore diverse approaches to expression, centering the experiences of refugee students and their families.
2. Create arts-based narrative projects that provide safe, alternative channels for students to share their experiences and build resilience.
3. Design inclusive resources that celebrate multiple forms of communication and storytelling across different cultural contexts.
4. Establish collaborative partnerships between educational institutions and refugee support organizations to develop culturally responsive communication support strategies.
5. Create community programs that recognize and value alternative forms of communication and expression.

References

Al Rawi, S. (2018). *The Baghdad clock: Winner of the Edinburgh First Book Award.* Oneworld Publications.

Al-Ali, N. (2013). *Iraqi women untold stories from 1948 to the present.* Bloomsbury Publishing

Antoon, S. (2010). *The corpse washer.* Yale University Press.

Antoon, S. (2019). *The book of collateral damage (The Margellos World Republic of Letters).* Yale University Press.

Ellis, D. (2009). *Children of war: Voices of Iraqi refugees.* Groundwood Books.

Kadri, A. (2007). *The orange trees of Baghdad.* Key Porter Books.

Vaughan, B. K. (2006). *Pride of Baghdad.* Vertigo.

CHAPTER FIVE

Adam and Aya:

Third-Generation Palestinian Refugee Siblings Navigating Cerebral Palsy and Epilepsy in Baddawi Refugee Camp

Background

Adam and Aya are Palestinian siblings growing up in the Baddawi refugee camp in Lebanon, a settlement that was established to provide shelter for Palestinians who fled violence and displacement generations ago. Born in the camp, they carry the legacy of their parents and grandparents, who also spent their lives within its borders. Their identities as third-generation refugees are significantly shaped by the oral narratives and collective memories passed down through their family and community, framing their understanding of being Palestinian. The camp serves not only as their home but as a symbol of a protracted conflict that has denied their people the right to return to their ancestral lands.

Adam and Aya's paternal grandparents, Mohammad and Fatima, originally hailed from a small village near Hebron. Mohammad worked as a farmer, cultivating olives and citrus fruits, while Fatima managed the household and took care of their young children. Life in Hebron was marked by strong community ties, vibrant cultural traditions, and a deep connection to the land. However, the occupation of Palestine and the outbreak of violence and subsequent displacement in the late 1940s forced them to flee their home. With only the possessions they could carry, they embarked on a difficult journey northward, seeking safety and refuge. Their journey was arduous, filled with uncertainty and hardship. They traveled by foot and by whatever transportation they could find, eventually reaching Lebanon.

Upon arrival, they found themselves in a temporary refugee camp, which gradually became a more permanent settlement. Despite the challenges, they remained resilient, preserving their cultural heritage and passing it on to their children.

Their maternal grandparents, Ali and Leila, had a similar journey. Ali, a skilled carpenter, and Leila, a talented seamstress, brought their skills with them to Lebanon. They used these talents to contribute to the growing refugee community, building shelters and creating clothing that maintained traditional Palestinian patterns and designs. Both sets of grandparents faced significant challenges in adapting to life in Lebanon but remained steadfast in their commitment to their cultural identity and hope for a better future. Their stories of resilience and perseverance became an integral part of the family's legacy, influencing Adam and Aya's understanding of their heritage and their place in the world.

The Baddawi refugee camp was established in the early 1950s as a temporary solution to house the influx of Palestinian refugees fleeing conflict. The Lebanese people, despite their own economic and social challenges, showed remarkable generosity in hosting and supporting the displaced Palestinians. The camp was initially intended to provide short-term shelter, but over time, it evolved into a more permanent settlement as the conflict persisted and a resolution remained elusive.

The formation and maintenance of the camp presented numerous general challenges. The infrastructure was not designed to support long-term habitation, leading to issues such as frequent electricity outages, limited access to clean water, and inadequate sanitation facilities. The camp's layout, with narrow pathways, uneven surfaces, and multi-level structures, was not conducive to accessibility, posing significant barriers for individuals with mobility impairments like Adam.

Life in the Refugee Camp

Life in the Baddawi camp is marked by significant hardships that affect every aspect of daily living. The camp's infrastructure struggles to meet the basic needs of its residents. Frequent electricity outages disrupt daily routines, making it difficult to study, work, or even cook. Limited access to clean water poses health risks and complicates personal hygiene and household chores. The lack of proper sanitation facilities leads to unsanitary conditions, contributing to the spread of diseases.

Economically, opportunities are scarce. The few available jobs, such as construction labor for men and embroidery work for women, offer meager incomes that barely cover essential expenses. The cost of living remains high, with basic necessities like food and medicine often out of reach for many families. The camp's dense population and cramped living conditions further exacerbate these challenges, creating a stressful and often unhealthy environment.

Despite these difficulties, the community remains resilient. The camp's residents have developed informal support systems to help each other navigate these challenges. Neighbors share resources, and extended families often live close together, providing mutual support. Community leaders and organizations work tirelessly to improve living conditions and advocate for better services.

Palestinian culture, marked by strong connections to family and community, thrives even in adversity. The concept of "Sumud," which means steadfastness, embodies the resilience of the Palestinian people, a resilience the siblings witness daily as stories of endurance and hope circulate within their community. Additionally, storytelling becomes an essential instrument for preserving their cultural heritage and the collective dream of returning to their homeland. This foundation shapes their views and aspirations, providing a sense of continuity and purpose amid the uncertainties they face.

Adam: Navigating Physical Disability

Adam's physical disability resulted from complications during his birth when access to adequate medical care was delayed at a checkpoint. The resulting cerebral palsy affects primarily his lower limbs, requiring him to use crutches for mobility. In the camp's early years, it was designed as a temporary housing solution with narrow pathways, uneven surfaces, and multiple steps between sections, all features that present significant barriers for someone with mobility impairments. As the camp evolved into a permanent settlement, some pathways were widened and paved, but accessibility was never a consideration in its development, reflecting both resource limitations and the broader societal neglect of disability needs.

Social interactions at school are complicated by the stigma surrounding his disability. Adam faces exclusion and bullying from some peers, while others mistakenly perceive him as incapable. These dynamics challenge Adam's sense of agency as he works to assert his independence against a backdrop of misunderstanding. Nevertheless, he ultimately cultivates meaningful relationships with a close-knit group of friends who recognize and celebrate his strengths. Together, they dream and aspire to carve out futures that transcend the limitations imposed by the camp.

Aya: Managing Invisible Disability

Aya, Adam's older sister, faces different challenges with her epilepsy, diagnosed when she was 6 years old after experiencing her first seizure during a family gathering. The diagnosis process was difficult due to limited neurological specialists in the region. For 2 years, her seizures were misattributed to childhood anxiety related to the stresses of camp life. By age 8, her parents finally secured a proper diagnosis through a traveling medical team, but medication options were limited and often inconsistently available due to restrictions on medical imports.

Despite these challenges, Aya has developed into a successful student who enjoys traditional embroidery, spending time with her cousins, and excels in mathematics and Arabic literature. Her community has developed informal support systems for managing her condition; neighbors know to call her parents if they notice seizure activity, and extended family members are trained to provide basic seizure first aid. This communal safety net gives Aya a degree of independence despite her medical condition.

Intersections of Disability and Refugee Experience

The siblings' experiences highlight how disability intersects with their status as Palestinian refugees in Lebanon, creating layered challenges but also fostering unique strengths and resilience.

For Adam, his physical disability and the camp's inaccessible environment create daily obstacles to mobility and independence. The narrow pathways, uneven terrain, and multi-level structures of the camp, designed as temporary housing but now a permanent settlement, present significant barriers. His disability experience is inseparable from the spatial limitations of the refugee camp. Where a child with similar mobility challenges in a different context might have access to accessible buildings and pathways, Adam navigates a physical environment never designed with disability in mind. Yet his daily navigation of these spaces has cultivated remarkable problem-solving skills and adaptability.

For Aya, managing epilepsy in a setting with limited medical resources creates constant uncertainty. Medication shortages due to import restrictions, the scarcity of neurological specialists, and the difficulty of maintaining regular treatment schedules during periods of heightened tensions all complicate her condition management. The unpredictability of her medical care mirrors the broader unpredictability of refugee life, creating compounded challenges. Rather than having the stable medical support that might be available elsewhere, her seizure management requires improvisation and community vigilance. Yet these challenges have fostered in her a deep awareness of her body's signals and an ability to advocate for her needs within supportive community networks.

Both siblings benefit from the collective orientation of Palestinian society in the camp, where community support networks provide essential safety nets. For Adam, this means neighbors who help navigate difficult terrain or carry items when needed; for Aya, it means an extended community trained to recognize and respond appropriately to seizure activity.

Educational Experiences and Adaptations

Both Adam and Aya attend UNRWA (United Nations Relief and Works Agency) schools in the camp, where resource limitations create significant challenges for accommodating their different disabilities. Unlike formal special education systems in countries like the United States, the camp's educational environment lacks structured processes for identifying, evaluating, and supporting students with disabilities.

Despite these challenges, both siblings have developed effective adaptation strategies in the absence of formal special education structures. Adam excels in subjects that don't require physical activity, particularly history and literature, where his storytelling abilities shine. He has developed upper body strength that allows him to navigate the camp with increasing independence and uses his understanding of the camp's layout to plan efficient routes that avoid the most inaccessible areas.

Family Dynamics and Support Systems

The siblings' parents play crucial roles that parallel many functions of special education teams in formalized systems. Without access to the structured evaluation and eligibility determination processes available in countries like the United States, they have created their own systems for identifying needs, documenting progress, and implementing accommodations.

Their father functions simultaneously as case manager, advocate, and assistive technology specialist. He uses his limited free time to create adaptive tools for Adam, including a customized desk that accommodates his seating needs and storage solutions that keep necessary items within reach. These innovations would typically be provided through an IEP's related services in formal special education systems. For Aya, he maintains meticulous records of her seizure activity and medication effects, creating documentation that helps identify triggers and treatment efficacy despite the lack of consistent neurological care. These records serve functions similar to the data collection required for developing appropriate accommodations in formal IEPs.

Their mother incorporates both children's needs into her daily routines, planning neighborhood activities that Adam can access and teaching Aya embroidery techniques that help manage stress, a significant seizure trigger. She has become an informal educator within the community, discreetly correcting misconceptions about both children's conditions while maintaining the family's dignity. This community education role addresses functions that would be served by disability awareness programs and professional development for staff in more formalized educational settings.

The siblings themselves have developed a supportive relationship that bridges their different experiences of disability. Adam helps track Aya's medication schedule and recognizes subtle signs of impending seizures that even their parents sometimes miss. Aya advocates for her brother in social situations, challenging exclusion and highlighting his capabilities rather than limitations. Together, they navigate the physical and social landscape of the camp with complementary strengths and awareness of each other's vulnerabilities.

Extended family members and neighbors form an additional layer of support that fulfills functions often assigned to specialized professionals in formal special education systems. Cousins include Adam in games adapted to accommodate his mobility, creating informal versions of adaptive physical education. An uncle who works occasionally as an electrician ensures their home receives priority during power restoration after outages, knowing Aya's seizure medication must be refrigerated. Neighbors share information about visiting medical teams that might provide specialized care, creating an informal referral network similar to the procedural safeguards in formal systems that ensure access to appropriate evaluations and services.

Community religious leaders have worked to counter stigmatizing beliefs about both disabilities, providing psychosocial support that might come from school counselors or social workers in formalized education systems. This community-based approach to disability support differs significantly from the individualized focus of special education eligibility processes in countries like the United States, reflecting different cultural values and adaptations to resource limitations.

Dreams and Aspirations Amid Constraints

Despite the significant constraints of both their disabilities and their status as Palestinian refugees in Lebanon, Adam and Aya maintain powerful aspirations for their futures, though they recognize the stark contrast between their current educational support and what might be available elsewhere.

Their parents have increasingly discussed the possibility of relocation to the United States, where formal disability support systems might provide opportunities unavailable in the camp. The family has begun gathering information about American special education rights, researching the evaluation processes they would need to navigate and connecting with other Palestinian families who have made similar transitions. While excited about the potential access to specialized services, assistive technology, and educational accommodations, they also worry about the challenges of navigating an unfamiliar system in a new language and culture.

Resilience and Cultural Identity

For both Adam and Aya, Palestinian cultural identity provides essential resources for resilience amid the challenges of disability and displacement.

Traditional storytelling practices, preserved through oral history and community gatherings, offer them narratives of persistence through hardship that resonate with their own experiences. Family stories of ancestors who overcame significant obstacles provide templates for understanding their own struggles within a longer historical arc. When community elders recount tales of survival and adaptation across generations of displacement, both siblings find frameworks for contextualizing their own challenges. The siblings particularly connect with Palestinian cultural emphasis on education as both resistance and preservation, finding purpose in academic achievement despite significant barriers.

Islamic perspectives within their community offer additional frameworks for understanding disability that counter potential stigma. While some community members initially viewed both conditions through supernatural lenses, family and religious leaders emphasized interpretations focusing on community responsibility to support those with different abilities, positioning disability as an opportunity for collective care rather than individual burden. Religious teachings about patience in adversity and community solidarity provide spiritual resources that complement medical and educational approaches to disability management.

Through these cultural resources, Adam and Aya develop identities that integrate their experiences of disability into their understanding of being Palestinian rather than positioning these aspects of experience in opposition. Their resilience emerges not despite their cultural context but through the resources it provides for meaning-making and community support amid significant challenges. In a context where formal support systems are limited, cultural frameworks for understanding adversity and adaptation become essential tools for navigating both disability and displacement.

Accessing Special Education Services When Relocation Happens

Initial Steps for Accessing Services

Enrollment and Language Assessment: Upon arrival, the family would first enroll both children in their local public school. As English language learners, Adam and Aya would likely undergo language proficiency assessment to determine appropriate language support services.

Comprehensive Evaluation: Both children would undergo comprehensive evaluations by a multidisciplinary team. Adam would likely be evaluated by physical and occupational therapists to assess his mobility needs, as well as educational assessments to determine any academic impacts of his cerebral palsy. Aya would need neurological documentation of her epilepsy, potentially including EEG studies and assessments to determine how seizure activity affects her learning.

Challenges and Opportunities During This Process

Documentation Challenges: The family would face significant challenges providing standard medical documentation from their years in the refugee camp. Neurological reports for Aya's epilepsy and developmental history for Adam's cerebral palsy might be incomplete or in formats unfamiliar to American schools. The father's meticulous personal records would be invaluable but might not be recognized as "official" documentation without translation and authentication.

Strengths and Resources: Despite these challenges, the family brings significant strengths to this process. Their detailed observations and innovative accommodations demonstrate deep understanding of their children's needs. Their experience advocating within limited systems has developed their persistence and problem-solving skills. Their cultural perspective on disability as integrated with identity rather than deficit-based offers a valuable counterbalance to clinical approaches.

Potential Services and Accommodations

If successfully navigated, the special education system could provide significant benefits for both children:

For Adam: Physical and occupational therapy services would be available to improve his mobility and independence. Assistive technology for mobility and academics would help overcome physical barriers. Accessible transportation to and from school would ensure consistent attendance. A modified physical education program would allow appropriate participation.

For Aya: A healthcare plan for seizure management at school would be developed with medical professionals. Staff training in seizure response would ensure appropriate care during incidents. Academic accommodations for missed content during seizure activity would maintain educational progress. Extended time for assignments and assessments would account for processing fluctuations.

Conclusion

Adam and Aya's story illustrates the complex intersections of disability, refugee status, and cultural identity. Their experiences highlight how disability manifests differently within the constraints of refugee camp settings, yet also demonstrates the remarkable resilience and adaptability that emerges through family and community support systems.

As their family contemplates potential relocation to environments with formalized disability services, their experiences raise important questions about how special education systems might better recognize and build upon the cultural strengths, family knowledge, and innovative accommodations already developed by refugee families. Adam and Aya's story ultimately demonstrates that effective disability support transcends standardized processes and resource availability. It emerges through the creative integration of cultural knowledge, community engagement, and family advocacy. These are elements that could strengthen both informal educational accommodations in refugee settings and formal special education systems in more resourced environments.

Discussion Questions

Understanding Disability in Refugee Contexts

1. How does the Baddawi refugee camp's physical environment impact Adam and Aya's experiences of disability differently? What creative solutions might improve accessibility in such low-resource environments?

2. Consider the intersection of refugee identity and disability. How might Adam and Aya's experiences of exclusion and discrimination based on their disabilities mirror or differ from the collective experiences of Palestinians in exile?

3. How do visible disabilities (like Adam's cerebral palsy) and invisible disabilities (like Aya's epilepsy) create different challenges in a refugee camp setting? How might support systems address both types effectively?

4. What role does the concept of "Sumud" (steadfastness) play in how the siblings and their family understand and manage disability? How does this cultural concept influence their resilience?

5. Compare and contrast the informal disability support systems in Baddawi camp with formal special education processes (like those outlined in IDEA). What are the advantages and disadvantages of each approach?

Educational Implications and Strategies

1. What approaches might educators use to identify and address the different accommodation needs for students like Adam (mobility challenges) and Aya (seizure management) in settings with limited resources? How could elements of formal eligibility evaluation processes be adapted for refugee contexts?

2. Consider the 13 disability categories under IDEA in the United States. How might these formal classifications help or hinder understanding of Adam and Aya's educational needs in their context? What alternative classification systems might better serve refugee educational settings?

3. How might an Individualized Education Program (IEP) process be adapted for use in refugee camp schools? What cultural modifications would make such formal documentation processes more effective and culturally appropriate?

4. What multimodal approaches to instruction can leverage both siblings' cultural strengths while accommodating their different disability-related challenges? How can these approaches be implemented without the specialized resources typically available in formal special education settings?

5. How might educators create appropriate assessment accommodations for students like Adam and Aya without access to formal evaluation data or specialized assessment tools? What principles from special education assessment could be adapted for low-resource environments?

Community and Cultural Resources

1. How does the family's approach to disability management reflect both traditional Palestinian cultural values and adaptation to limited medical resources?

2. What role does storytelling and collective memory play in Adam and Aya's education and identity development? How might educators leverage these cultural resources to support learning?

3. How might traditional practices (like embroidery for Aya) be incorporated into formal therapeutic approaches for students with similar conditions in educational settings?

4. How can schools partner with community resources and organizations to improve accessibility and inclusion for students with different types of disabilities in refugee camp settings?

5. In what ways do the siblings' different disabilities affect their connection to cultural traditions and practices? How might cultural activities be adapted to be more inclusive?

Future Directions for Research and Practice

1. What specific trauma-informed approaches need to be developed for students who have experienced both conflict-related displacement and ongoing disability challenges? How might these approaches differ from standard special education practices?

2. How could the procedural safeguards and parental rights aspects of formal special education systems be adapted to empower refugee families advocating for their children with disabilities?

3. What transitional approaches might help students like Adam and Aya if they relocated to countries with formal special education systems? How could educators bridge gaps between informal accommodations and standardized eligibility processes?

4. How might special education eligibility evaluation tools need to be modified to accurately assess refugee students with disabilities, accounting for educational gaps, cultural differences, and trauma impacts?

5. How can the family-driven informal accommodation approaches developed in refugee settings inform improvements to formal special education systems, potentially making them more culturally responsive and family centered?

References

Abdelrazaq, L. (2015). *Baddawi*. Just World Books.

Alyan, H. (2017). *Salt houses*. Houghton Mifflin Harcourt.

Barakat, I. (2016). *Balcony on the moon: Coming of age in Palestine*. Farrar, Straus and Giroux.

Bigelow, B., Hagopian, J., Kassouf, S., Sanchez, A., & Shoman, S. (Eds.). (2025). *Teaching Palestine: Lessons, stories, voices.* Rethinking Schools.

Bsharat, A. (2017). *Code name: Butterfly* (N. Marston, Trans.). Neem Tree Press.

Dunsky, M. (2023). *Stories from Palestine: Narratives of resilience.* University of Notre Dame Press.

Fahed, N., & Saftner, P. (Eds.). (2021). *11 lives: Stories from Palestinian exiles.* Institute for Palestine Studies & OR Books.

Jarrar, R. (2009). *A map of home.* Penguin Books.

CHAPTER SIX

Maha's Journey:

Supporting Students with Visual Impairment in Inclusive Classrooms

Background

MAHA MUAMBA IS MORE than an individual navigating the challenges of visual impairment and displacement; she is the heart of a remarkable family whose collective resilience transforms potential limitations into extraordinary opportunities. At 15 years old, Maha represents the complex intersection of disability, forced migration, and unwavering familial support.

The Muamba family hails from Goma in eastern Democratic Republic of Congo, a region marked by persistent conflict and extraordinary challenges. Her father, Jean-Pierre Muamba, worked as a dedicated schoolteacher, while her mother, Marie Muamba, ran a vibrant market stall selling locally crafted fabrics. Their family dynamic was characterized by deep love, mutual support, and an unshakeable commitment to each other's potential.

Beyond Maha, the Muamba household bustled with the energy of three younger siblings, each bringing their unique strengths to the family's collective journey:

Kiza Muamba, the 12-year-old middle son, emerged as Maha's most steadfast ally. Bright and protective, he developed an extraordinary ability to assist his sister without undermining her independence. During their most challenging moments of displacement, Kiza would help Maha navigate difficult terrain, describe surroundings, and fiercely defend her against those who would underestimate her capabilities. His passion for mathematics and problem-solving often translated into creative solutions for Maha's accessibility challenges.

Amani Muamba, the 9-year-old daughter, harbored dreams of becoming a doctor. Her early fascination with medical care made her an intuitive support for Maha. She would meticulously describe visual information, helping Maha build mental maps of new environments. Amani's compassionate nature and intellectual curiosity meant she was always seeking ways to support her sister's educational and sensory development.

The youngest, Bahati Muamba, was a 6-year-old bundle of creativity and imagination. Despite his young age, Bahati developed a profound understanding of his sister's experiences. He would create elaborate stories where Maha was always the hero, transforming her visual impairment into sources of strength. His storytelling became a powerful form of emotional support, helping Maha reframe her experiences through narratives of resilience and possibility.

This family's approach to Maha's visual impairment was revolutionary. Rather than viewing her condition as a limitation, they celebrated it as a unique aspect of her identity. Jean-Pierre and Marie consistently challenged societal stigma, advocating for Maha's inclusion in community life and educational opportunities. They refused to allow traditional misconceptions about disability to define their daughter's potential.

Brief History of Wars in the Congo

The Democratic Republic of Congo has endured devastating armed conflicts that have profoundly shaped the lives of its citizens. The First Congo War (1996–1997) erupted after decades of misrule under Mobutu Sese Seko, with Rwandan and Ugandan forces supporting rebel leader Laurent-Désiré Kabila to overthrow the government. This conflict was quickly followed by the Second Congo War (1998–2003), often called "Africa's World War," which involved nine African nations and resulted in approximately 5.4 million deaths, primarily from disease and starvation.

Despite a formal peace agreement in 2003, eastern Congo, particularly North and South Kivu provinces where the Muamba family lived, continued to suffer from persistent violence. Multiple armed groups, including the FDLR (Democratic Forces for the Liberation of Rwanda), various Mai-Mai militias, and M23 rebels have perpetuated cycles of conflict. Mineral resource exploitation, ethnic tensions, and weak governance created conditions where violence became normalized.

For civilians in eastern Congo, particularly those with disabilities like Maha, these conflicts meant constant insecurity, disrupted education, limited access to healthcare, and eventually, forced displacement. Schools were frequently targets of attacks or recruitment sites for child soldiers, making education dangerous and inconsistent. Medical facilities were overwhelmed with trauma cases, leaving little capacity for specialized care for conditions like visual impairment.

The conflict directly impacted the availability of medical supplies, including the medications and specialized equipment Maha needed. International aid organizations struggled to maintain consistent services in volatile security environments, creating gaps in care that had lasting consequences for many disabled children.

Early Life in Congo and Disability Experience

Born with congenital glaucoma in Goma, Democratic Republic of Congo, Maha's early years featured more obstacles than opportunities. Her condition caused progressive vision loss that by age 5 had reduced her sight to perceiving only light, shadows, and some large shapes in her right eye, while her left eye had no light perception. Navigating her environment required developing extraordinary compensatory skills, with daily activities demanding conscious effort and planning. Her world was shaped by conflict, limited medical resources, and unwavering family support. Regular ophthalmological care was largely unavailable, and existing medical care focused primarily on conflict-related injuries. Her parents, Jean-Pierre and Marie, refused to let societal barriers limit their daughter's potential.

Maha's visual impairment presented significant challenges in a conflict zone with limited specialized resources. Without proper early intervention or regular access to ophthalmologists, her glaucoma progressed more rapidly than it might have with consistent treatment. Local facilities lacked pediatric low vision services, proper optical devices, or specialists in childhood visual impairment. Medications to control intraocular pressure were inconsistently available and expensive. Despite these challenges, Maha's cognitive development progressed normally, and she demonstrated exceptional verbal abilities and auditory memory.

Their small home became a sanctuary of learning, where disability was reframed as a unique perspective rather than a limitation. When local schools rejected Maha, citing insufficient resources for blind students, her parents transformed their living room into a classroom. Jean-Pierre taught lessons, building her listening skills, verbal expression, and imagination, while Marie created tactile learning materials from household items: bottle caps became counting tools, fabric scraps formed textured alphabets, and homemade reliefs helped Maha understand spatial concepts. By age 8, through this immersive home education, Maha developed remarkable spatial memory and auditory processing abilities, compensating for her vision loss with heightened awareness of sound, texture, and mental mapping of physical spaces.

Navigating Physical Barriers in Conflict-Affected Goma

Goma was unforgiving for someone with visual impairment. Unpaved roads with sudden drops, debris-filled pathways, and constantly changing routes due to conflict created a hostile environment for independent mobility. Unexploded ordinances dotted nearby fields, and distant conflict sounds were constant. For Maha, navigation was a daily negotiation, each movement demonstrating resilience. Her acute hearing, memory for routes, and family support became her primary survival tools, teaching her that adaptation is a form of strength. When Jean-Pierre brought Maha to public spaces, environmental barriers were overwhelming. Lack of tactile markers, inconsistent pathways, and unpredictable obstacles excluded her from community life. Public transportation was chaotic and dangerous, forcing the family to carefully guide Maha when traveling beyond walking distance. These environmental barriers reinforced societal attitudes viewing disability as a private family matter rather than a community responsibility.

During this period, Maha developed exceptional sensory compensation skills. Her hearing became remarkably acute, allowing her to identify individuals by their footsteps and gauge distances through echo location. She became adept at problem-solving environmental challenges, mentally mapping spaces through touch and sound. This spatial awareness and tactical thinking became cognitive strengths that would later translate to academic contexts.

Deteriorating Conditions and Displacement

The decision to leave came after increasing danger. Targeted attacks near their community made staying too risky. Collecting refugee documentation became complex, with lost papers and fractured records, further complicated by the need to document Maha's medical condition with limited access to healthcare records or specialists. Their escape to neighboring Uganda posed extraordinary challenges for Maha, whose visual impairment made navigating unfamiliar and dangerous terrain particularly hazardous. Throughout the journey, her family members took turns describing surroundings and guiding her across treacherous paths, while Maha relied on her walking stick and acute hearing to detect obstacles. The family left behind most adaptive equipment, including tactile learning materials, specialized writing tools, and audio devices that had supported her learning.

In the refugee settlement, they joined thousands of Congolese refugees in precarious conditions. Medical facilities offered only basic treatments, with specialized care for visual impairment virtually nonexistent. Marie became Maha's primary guide, sensory support, and intellectual advocate. The refugee camp introduced new challenges for managing Maha's condition. Constantly changing layouts and crowded pathways created disorienting environments. Communal facilities lacked any accommodations for the visually impaired, forcing Marie to develop alternative navigation strategies. Without proper medical care, Maha's intraocular pressure remained unmanaged, potentially causing further vision deterioration.

During 18 months in Uganda, Maha's educational progress slowed. While informal education existed in the camp, most occurred in visually dependent formats without accommodations. Jean-Pierre continued teaching whenever possible, focusing on oral language acquisition and storytelling. Despite challenges, Maha developed remarkable listening comprehension and memory skills, mentally cataloging stories, facts, and languages with exceptional retention.

The Refugee Resettlement Process

The refugee resettlement process revealed harsh bureaucratic realities. Their application to the United States was a 3-year journey of hope, uncertainty, and advocacy. Each interview and medical screening risked rejection. Maha's visual impairment was frequently reduced to medical reports, her potential overlooked. Immigration officials questioned whether her disability would place "undue burden" on the United States' healthcare system, requiring additional documentation demonstrating her cognitive capabilities. Throughout this process, Maha had almost no access to ophthalmological care or low vision services. By age 12, what minimal vision she had retained continued to diminish without proper medical intervention. Yet her linguistic abilities flourished. She became fluent in Swahili, Lingala, and some Luganda and was rapidly learning English from volunteers and aid organization materials. The family received pre-departure cultural orientation about the American educational system, but with almost no information about disability services or accommodations. They arrived with limited understanding of their rights to assistive technology, educational support, or medical services, significantly impacting their first resettlement year.

Arrival and Adaptation in the United States

Their new home was not the promised land they imagined. Their initial housing was disorienting for Maha, with unfamiliar layouts and no tactile markers, creating daily navigational challenges. The family's journey toward accessing support services revealed complex bureaucracy for refugee families with disabilities. Obtaining assistive technology tested their persistence. Insurance applications faced repeated rejection, each form requiring translations, medical verifications, and endless calls through a discouraging system. A simple request for a screen reader became a months-long advocacy journey, with Jean-Pierre and Marie meticulously documenting interactions, translating records, and navigating an unfamiliar healthcare system. When the screen reader arrived, it presented new challenges. A 6-week training period with a specialized expert was required to learn its interface, and school technology infrastructure proved inconsistent. Some classrooms lacked compatibility to support her adaptive technology, creating additional obstacles.

During their first month in their new home, Maha received her first professional ophthalmological assessment in years. Doctors diagnosed advanced glaucoma with complete blindness in her left eye and only minimal light perception remaining in her right eye. The prognosis was that her remaining vision could not be restored, but proper care could prevent further deterioration. Comprehensive medical support revealed both the permanence of her vision loss and new adaptation possibilities. Maha received her first proper white cane and orientation and mobility training 3 months after arrival, dramatically increasing her independence. This training transformation coincided with improved confidence as she learned to navigate American environments more independently. For the first time, Maha could travel within limited routes without constant family guidance. Their initial interactions with the American healthcare system were mixed. While care quality and resources exceeded previous access, cultural and linguistic barriers created challenges. Medical appointments often lacked appropriate interpreters, leaving parents struggling to understand treatment recommendations or describe Maha's needs. Healthcare providers sometimes made culturally inappropriate suggestions, failing to recognize how the family's experiences shaped their perspective on disability management.

Educational Experience in the United States

Maha's educational journey began with significant challenges. Initial assessments focused on English proficiency and standardized measures that failed to capture her intellectual capabilities. Despite advanced reasoning skills and multilingual abilities, she was placed in classes below her cognitive level based primarily on limited English and assumptions about her visual impairment.

Special Education Eligibility in the American School System

Upon arriving in the United States, the Muamba family encountered a complex special education qualification process. The Individuals with Disabilities Education Act (IDEA) provides the framework for special education services in American schools, requiring that students receive evaluations to determine eligibility. For Maha, this process began when her parents requested an evaluation through their local school district.

Under IDEA, Maha would need to meet two key criteria to qualify for special education services: having one of the 13 disability categories identified in the law, and requiring specialized instruction as a result. Visual impairment, including blindness, is explicitly named as one of these qualifying conditions. The law defines visual impairment as "an impairment in vision that, even with correction, adversely affects a child's educational performance."

The evaluation process included:

1. A comprehensive assessment by a multidisciplinary team
2. Vision assessments confirming her medical diagnosis

3. Educational testing to determine how her visual impairment impacted her learning
4. An assessment of her need for specialized instruction and related services

The evaluation confirmed that Maha qualified under the visual impairment category. Her Individualized Education Program (IEP) team, which included her parents, general education teacher, special education teacher, vision specialist, and school administrator, then developed an educational plan.

The IEP process revealed both supports and challenges. The team determined that Maha required:

1. Instruction from a teacher of the visually impaired
2. Orientation and mobility services
3. Assistive technology including screen readers and braille materials
4. Extended time for assignments and tests
5. Alternative formats for visual materials

However, bureaucratic hurdles and limited experience with refugee students with disabilities created delays. The school initially lacked translated materials explaining parental rights under IDEA, compounding the family's confusion about the process. Jean-Pierre and Marie struggled to fully participate in IEP meetings without consistent translation services, sometimes relying on Kiza to interpret complex educational terminology.

Once her eligibility was established, Maha began receiving services from a teacher of the visually impaired who visited twice weekly. However, the initial IEP goals underestimated her intellectual capabilities, focusing primarily on basic skills rather than challenging academic content. Through persistent advocacy and as Maha's English skills improved, the team eventually revised her goals to better reflect her capabilities.

Maha's first school initially lacked basic accessibility accommodations. Classrooms lacked tactile markers or consistent organization, and the school relied on sighted guides rather than addressing fundamental accessibility issues. Reading materials were often provided in inaccessible formats, requiring last-minute conversions that delayed Maha's access to content. The assessment process for developing accommodations moved slowly, complicated by language barriers, lack of medical records, and limited staff experience with visual impairment in multilingual students. What might have taken weeks for a local student stretched into months. During this period, Maha's parents struggled to navigate an unfamiliar educational system without understanding their accommodation rights or relevant processes.

Maha found sanctuary in unexpected places. The local library became a portal to possibility. A compassionate librarian recognized something special in Maha, connecting her with transformative supplementary programs. The library provided auditory learning resources and accessible technology where Maha could work without visual strain, becoming her primary study location. Mr. Thompson, her social studies teacher, was the first educator to see her potential beyond visual limitations. Rather than focusing on limitations, he identified her exceptional analytical thinking and communication potential. He advocated for appropriate academic challenges regardless of her English development stage, recognizing that cognitive engagement could accelerate language acquisition. Under Mr. Thompson's mentorship and after months developing an appropriate support plan, Maha began recording powerful oral essays examining refugee experiences, drawing from personal history with depth that surprised her teachers. This academic success shifted how school staff perceived her, from viewing her primarily as a student with visual impairment to recognizing her as an intellectually gifted learner with unique perspectives. This perceptual shift resulted in tangible program changes, including placement in advanced courses with appropriate accessibility accommodations.

Assistive Technology and Accessibility Accommodations

When Maha's academic potential became apparent, the school's accommodation approach shifted significantly. Screen reading software and auditory learning tools became her academic lifeline, compensating for visual limitations that made traditional learning materials inaccessible. This technology transformed her educational experience, allowing access to content that accurately reflected her sophisticated thinking without previous barriers. Tactile markers throughout the school environment increased her mobility and independence. Alternative format materials, including braille and audio texts, allowed proper access to curriculum content that reduced frustration during long school days. These accessibility modifications addressed environmental barriers that had limited her participation, creating conditions where her cognitive abilities could take center stage. The adaptation process wasn't without setbacks. Initial technology solutions weren't always culturally or personally appropriate. Screen readers struggled with Maha's accent and multilingual vocabulary, causing frustration until more adaptive programs were identified. Some accommodations drew unwanted peer attention, creating social challenges that required thoughtful navigation by supportive teachers who helped normalize assistive technology within classroom culture.

Conclusion: Maha's Transformative Journey

Maha's story illuminates the extraordinary resilience of students navigating the complex intersections of disability, forced displacement, and educational adaptation. Her journey from the Democratic Republic of Congo to the United States represents a profound narrative of human potential, family support, and the transformative power of inclusive education. Fleeing conflict, navigating refugee camps, and ultimately resettling in the United States presented continuous challenges where each transition required reimagining access, education, and personal identity. Her educational experiences reveal both the significant barriers and remarkable possibilities of inclusive education, where initial misunderstandings about her capabilities gave way to recognition of her intellectual gifts. Supportive educators like Mr. Thompson became crucial allies, shifting perspectives from seeing sensory limitations to recognizing extraordinary analytical abilities.

Maha's story challenges us to reimagine educational spaces through approaches that recognize disability as human diversity, validate displaced students' experiences, create responsive learning environments, center student strengths, and build partnerships between educators, families, and communities. For educators, her narrative is both invitation and challenge to look beyond standardized assessments, listen deeply to students' experiences, and create learning spaces that honor the full humanity of every learner. Maha's journey demonstrates that resilience is about navigating challenges with dignity, creativity, and hope within educational ecosystems where every student can fully express their unique capabilities.

Questions for Teacher Educators

Contextual Understanding

1. How do conflict zones reshape access to education for students with visual impairments, and what innovative compensatory strategies emerge from these environments?
2. What strengths and adaptive skills develop from navigating without sight in resource-limited settings, and how can educators build upon these capabilities?
3. How do cultural understandings of visual impairment vary between Congolese contexts and Western educational frameworks, and how do these differences impact support strategies?
4. What specific trauma-informed approaches need to be developed for students who have experienced both conflict-related displacement and ongoing visual impairment management?
5. How do interrupted medical interventions during displacement create specific educational challenges for students with visual impairments, and what collaborative approaches between medical and educational professionals best address these needs?

Accessibility and Learning

1. What low-cost modifications can improve classroom accessibility for students with visual impairments in schools with limited resources?
2. How can auditory fatigue and processing needs of students with visual impairments be effectively accommodated within standard school schedules?
3. What alternative participation strategies can support meaningful engagement when visual limitations impact traditional classroom activities?
4. How do accessibility barriers indirectly impact cognitive learning experiences through information gaps, participation limitations, and psychological effects?

5. What transportation and mobility solutions can ensure students with visual impairments have equivalent access to field trips, community-based learning, and extracurricular activities?

Universal Design in Limited-Resource Contexts

1. How can multiple means of representation be implemented with minimal technology to accommodate students with visual impairments?
2. What sustainable peer support structures could enhance accessibility without overtaxing classmates or creating dependency relationships?
3. How might locally available materials be repurposed to create tactile learning tools in schools with limited specialized equipment?
4. What community knowledge systems might inform alternative approaches to accessibility beyond Western medical models?
5. How can curriculum be modified to reduce visual dependency while maintaining academic rigor?

Identity Development and Social Inclusion

1. How do intersecting identities of refugee status and visual impairment shape educational experiences and self-concept development?
2. What approaches can validate students' complex backgrounds while supporting the development of self-advocacy skills?
3. How can classrooms recognize the expertise that emerges from living with visual impairment rather than positioning disabled students only as recipients of accommodation?
4. What mechanisms perpetuate the exclusion of visually impaired students from social aspects of education, and how can these be addressed?
5. How can educators support positive disability identity while respecting cultural variations in how visual impairment is understood?

Community-Based Solutions

1. How can local vision rehabilitation resources support educational inclusion through collaborative planning between medical and educational professionals?

2. What role do families play in developing effective accessibility accommodations, and how can their expertise be incorporated into educational planning?

3. How can schools build reciprocal partnerships with refugee communities that recognize cultural strengths while addressing disability-related educational needs?

4. What community-driven approaches can address orientation, mobility, and accessibility barriers beyond the school campus?

5. How can assistive technology solutions be developed collaboratively with students and families to ensure cultural appropriateness and meaningful implementation?

References

Bola, J. J. (2018). *No place to call home*. OWN IT!

Dongala, E. (2005). *Johnny Mad Dog*. Farrar, Straus and Giroux.

Uwiringiyimana, S., & Pesta, A. (2017). *How dare the sun rise: Memoirs of a war child*. Katherine Tegen Books.

Yamusangie, F. K. (2003). *Full circle*. AuthorHouse UK.

CONCLUSION

Transformative Pathways:

Reimagining Education at the Intersection of Displacement and Disability

Dear Educator, As we reach the culmination of our shared journey, I invite you to pause and reflect on the profound landscape of possibility that lies before you. The stories we have explored are more than academic case studies or theoretical frameworks. They are living testimonies to the extraordinary resilience of human spirit, the transformative power of compassionate education, and the remarkable potential that emerges when we truly see and honor the full humanity of our students.

Our exploration has taken us deep into the complex worlds of refugee students with disabilities, students whose lives are characterized not by limitation, but by remarkable adaptation, strength, and hope. We have witnessed how displacement creates unique challenges, but more importantly, how these challenges can be transformed into pathways of profound learning and connection.

The journey of an inclusive educator is never about implementing a fixed set of strategies. It is about cultivating a way of seeing that recognizes the profound cultural wealth, unique strengths, and extraordinary capabilities that each student brings to the classroom. Your role extends far beyond traditional teaching. You become a bridge builder, a hope cultivator, a creator of spaces where belonging is not just promised but actively created through daily acts of compassion and genuine human connection.

Consider the remarkable resilience we have witnessed. From Amira navigating both physical disabilities and dyslexia after fleeing Bosnia, to Amir developing remarkable visual memory despite detention conditions that exacerbated his autism. From Zahra adapting to cognitive changes after traumatic brain injury in Rwanda, to Noor finding alternative expression through art when trauma silenced her voice in Iraq. From Adam and Aya creating mutual support systems as Palestinian refugees with cerebral palsy and epilepsy in Baddawi camp, to Maha's transformative journey from homemade mobility aids in Congo to academic success using proper visual impairment accommodations in American schools. These stories challenge us to look beyond deficit narratives. These students are not defined by their disabilities or displacement, but by their extraordinary capacity to adapt, learn, and thrive.

Cultural understanding emerges as a critical lens through which we must understand disability and educational support. Each family we encountered demonstrated profound wisdom in supporting their children, not through medical models of fixing or correcting, but through frameworks of unconditional love, practical adaptation, and holistic care. Amira's Bosnian Muslim family preserved their educational values despite war's disruption. Amir's Rohingya parents adapted religious and cultural practices to accommodate his autism in detention. Zahra's Rwandan family integrated traditional healing practices with Western approaches to brain injury. Noor's Iraqi family found ways to honor her silence while maintaining cultural traditions of verbal expression. Adam and Aya's Palestinian community implemented collective care approaches rooted in "sumud" (steadfastness). Maha's Congolese family transformed her visual impairment into unique perspectives on the world. Your challenge is to create educational environments that respect and integrate these rich cultural perspectives, recognizing that there are multiple valid ways of understanding disability, learning, and human potential.

The path of displacement creates unique vulnerabilities, particularly for students with disabilities. Healthcare disruptions, multiple relocations, and heightened risks of violence are not abstract concepts, but lived realities that demand comprehensive, compassionate responses. Amira's war injuries and dyslexia received only rudimentary care in besieged Sarajevo. Amir's autism went unrecognized in a system focused on detention rather than development. Zahra's brain injury recovery was compromised by inadequate medical care during her refugee journey from Rwanda. Noor's selective mutism was misunderstood in under-resourced camp schools after fleeing Iraq. Adam and Aya faced medication shortages and inaccessible facilities in Lebanon's Baddawi refugee camp. Maha's visual impairment deteriorated during years of displacement from Congo without proper ophthalmological care. Your work will require you to be more than an educator; you will be a protector, an advocate, a creator of safe spaces where students can fully express their capabilities.

Dignity and independence become central themes in supporting refugee students with disabilities. Each interruption of routine, each forced dependency, carries profound psychological impacts. Amira's struggle to maintain her identity as a capable learner despite physical disabilities and dyslexia. Amir's need for predictability and concrete information in an inherently uncertain asylum process. Zahra's frustration when her traumatic brain injury challenges were mistaken for language barriers. Noor's retreat into selective mutism as a way of maintaining control over her experiences. Adam's determination to navigate inaccessible camp environments independently despite his cerebral palsy. Maha's transformation when finally given appropriate assistive technology for her visual impairment after years of physical limitation. Your role is to create educational environments that restore agency, that provide supports which enhance rather than diminish independence, that recognize the whole person beyond their disability or refugee status.

The most effective educational approaches will be those that operate with true complexity and nuance. This means integrating trauma-informed practices with culturally responsive teaching. It means breaking down professional silos and creating collaborative systems that bring together language specialists, special educators, mental health professionals, and most importantly family and community members. It means seeing educational support as a holistic, integrated journey of human development. Each of our case studies demonstrated how fragmented approaches failed these students, while integrated, collaborative solutions created transformative possibilities.

Statistical realities are sobering. With only 68% of refugee children attending primary school and just 34% reaching secondary education, the work of inclusive education becomes an urgent moral imperative. But these numbers tell only part of the story. They do not capture the remarkable potential that emerges when appropriate supports are provided: the intellectual curiosity, the artistic talents, the mathematical insights, the extraordinary human capabilities that can flourish when we create genuinely inclusive environments.

Your commitment to this work is itself an act of hope. You are not just preparing to teach; you are preparing to create worlds of possibility for students who have often been marginalized, overlooked, or misunderstood. You will learn that true educational justice is built through daily acts of compassion: a moment of genuine listening, a recognition of a student's unique strength, a classroom environment that makes space for full human expression. Whether working with students like Amira navigating multiple disabilities, like Amir with autism spectrum disorder, like Zahra with traumatic brain injury, like Noor with selective mutism, like Adam and Aya managing cerebral palsy and epilepsy with limited resources, or like Maha with visual impairment requiring assistive technology, your approach will be guided by seeing each student's full humanity rather than focusing solely on their challenges.

Trust in the compassion that brought you to this profession. Trust in your ability to learn, to grow, to adapt. Trust in the extraordinary potential of the students you will serve. Your classrooms will become more than physical spaces; they will be sanctuaries of possibility, grounds where students can not only learn but truly be seen, valued, and empowered to shape their own futures.

The road ahead will not always be straightforward. There will be moments of challenge, complexity, and uncertainty. But you are now equipped with something far more powerful than a set of predetermined strategies. You have developed a way of seeing that honors the complete experiences of your students, a perspective that recognizes disability not as a limitation, but as a different way of moving through and understanding the world.

Carry with you the stories we have explored. Let them remind you that behind every educational statistic, every case study, there are real human beings with rich inner worlds, extraordinary capabilities, and profound experiences. Your work is about more than education. It is about humanity, connection, and the profound belief that every student deserves a space where they can truly belong and thrive.

As you step into your future classrooms, know that you carry with you not just knowledge, but a deep commitment to creating educational spaces of genuine understanding and transformation. The impact you will make is immeasurable, extending far beyond the immediate moment of teaching into the profound landscapes of human potential.

With profound respect, deep gratitude, and unwavering hope,

Sadia

ABOUT THE AUTHOR

DR. SADIA WARSI serves as Professor of Special Education at National Louis University, researching the intersection of refugee experiences and disabilities in education, the use of diverse children's literature in teacher preparation, and minority parent involvement in special education. Her international background spanning India, Iraq, Saudi Arabia, and Canada informs her approach to American educational systems. With degrees from the University of Manitoba, The American University, and a Ph.D. from the University of Illinois at Chicago, she instructs graduate students in special education and early childhood education, integrating cultural responsiveness with evidence-based practices. Her scholarly contributions address critical gaps in educational service delivery for students navigating both displacement and disability challenges. Through strategic partnerships with educational institutions, she develops inclusive methodologies that honor students' multifaceted identities. Her publication *Beyond Labels: Understanding Refugee Students with Disabilities in Educational Contexts* exemplifies her commitment to connecting refugee education with special education frameworks. The case studies presented therein establish pathways for creating responsive learning environments for uniquely positioned learners. Dr. Warsi's work demonstrates her dedication to educational equity and her conviction that inclusive practices benefit the entire educational community.

INDEX